LIVE THE STORY

ヤルダ・ハキーム	ジョン・ソベル	リズ・デュセット	スティーヴン・サッカー	リンダ・ユエ
プレゼンター ＆ 特派員	プレゼンター	国際ニュース特派員チーフ	プレゼンター	ビジネス特派員チーフ

世界のどの報道局よりも多くのジャーナリストを世界各国に擁するBBCは、世界中のあらゆるニュースを迅速に、かつ正確にお伝えしています。まるでその場にいるかのような臨場感のあるニュースをお伝えできるよう日々努力している我々の報道にどうぞご期待ください。

———— BBCワールドニュース

お近くのケーブルテレビ、スカパー！、ひかりTVなどでご覧いただけます。

BBCワールドニュースの最新の番組スケジュール、メールマガジン登録など、詳しくはこちら

BBCワールドニュース 🔍 検索

BBC WORLD NEWS is a trademark of the British Broadcasting Corporation.© BBC 1996

Seeing the World through the News

2

Timothy Knowles
Daniel Brooks
Yukiko Takeoka
Mayumi Tamura
Rima Uraguchi

KINSEIDO

Kinseido Publishing Co., Ltd.
3-21 Kanda Jimbo-cho, Chiyoda-ku,
Tokyo 101-0051, Japan

Copyright© 2015 by Timothy Knowles
　　　　　　　　Daniel Brooks
　　　　　　　　Yukiko Takeoka
　　　　　　　　Mayumi Tamura
　　　　　　　　Rima Uraguchi

All rights reserved. No part of this publication may be reproduced, stored in a retrieval system, or transmitted, in any form or by any means, electronic, mechanical, photocopying, recording or otherwise, without the prior permission of the publisher.

First published 2015 by Kinseido Publishing Co., Ltd.

Cover design: parastyle inc.

News clips ©BBC 2014.
Images ©BBC 2014.
Cover images ©BBC 2014.

This edition produced under licence by Kinseido Publishing Co., Ltd. 2015.

BBCニュース ホームページ：www.bbcnews.com

Introduction

The British Broadcasting Corporation (BBC) is internationally famous for the quality and impartiality of its news items. BBC reporters also strive to make the news both interesting, and as easy to understand as possible. In this book we have chosen 15 items that we think would be of particular interest. Most are about Britain, as you might expect, but many of the issues covered, such as health, education and the environment are generally familiar to Japanese learners. There are also some important international issues, and topics that are included because they give a fascinating insight into a different culture.

It is hoped that the items will be motivating, and that students will be eager to watch and listen because they are interested in what they are discovering. New and important items of vocabulary are introduced, and the notes (in Japanese) will explain any interesting and important points of grammar and usage of English. However, perhaps the most important purpose of this book is that the learners should be able to engage in the subject matter, and then discuss it and research into it together. With this in mind, we have developed discussion questions that would encourage them to relate these new discoveries with what is already familiar to them in Japan.

We hope you enjoy the book.

はじめに

　本書は、BBCニュースを教材として、native speakerによりnatural speedで話される英語を通して、実際に起きている出来事について学び、英語力の向上を図ることを目指しています。また、イギリスをはじめとする世界各国の文化・社会についての知識も深めていきます。

　実際に放送されたBBCのニュースの中から、興味深いものだけを選りすぐり、分野も文化、社会から科学、環境まで多岐にわたり、幅広い知識が得られるよう心がけました。

　*Seeing the World through the News 1*に引き続き、ユニット内のコラムはイギリス文化についての面白い情報を増やして充実を図り、Questionsも最初のSetting the Sceneに始まりFollow Upに至るまで、各ユニットで取り上げるニュースを身近な問題として捉えられるよう配慮し、思わず話したくなるような内容となっております。活気溢れる授業となるよう、可能な限りの工夫をいたしました。

　本書を通じて、多民族国家イギリスが、4つの地域の独自性を保ちつつ、総体としてのイギリスらしさ（"Britishness"）を模索する今の姿を見ていただけると思います。また、古き良きイギリスの伝統、歴史、慣習と新しく生まれ変わるイギリスの両方についてバランス良く学んでいただけると考えています。

　最後になりましたが、本書の作成にあたり、BBCニュースを教材として使うことを許可して下さいましたBBCと、編集に際してご尽力いただきました金星堂の皆様に、この場をお借りして、心より感謝申し上げます。

　皆様が楽しんで笑顔で学んでいただけること、新しいことが学べる喜びと、以前よりも英語力がついたという自信、さらにもっと勉強してみようという意欲に少しでもつながるテキストになっていましたら、大変嬉しいです。

本書の使い方

テキストの特徴

　普段の生活の中で、ニュースの英語に触れる機会はあまりないかもしれません。本テキストは、初めて英語でニュースを観る場合でも無理なく取り組めるよう、多種多様なアクティビティを用意しています。単語のチェックや内容確認、穴埋め、要約、ディスカッションを通して、段階を踏みながらニュースを理解できるような作りになっているので、達成感を感じることができるでしょう。

Starting Off

1. Setting the Scene

　実際にニュースを観る前に、ニュースで扱われるトピックについて考えるためのセクションです。トピックについての学習を始めるにあたり、身近な問題としてトピックを捉えられるような問題を用意しました。ここで先にニュースに関する情報を整理しておけば、実際にニュースを観る際に理解が容易になります。ニュースで使われている単語や語句、または重要な概念をここで予習しておきましょう。

2. Building Language

　ニュースの中で使われる重要単語を学びます。単に日本語の訳語を覚えるのではなく、英語での定義を通して、また同義語を覚えながら、単語の持つ意味を英語で理解することを目指します。また、これらの単語はディスカッションを行うときにもおそらく頻繁に使うことになる単語ですし、ニュースの核となる単語ですので、発音もしっかりと確認することが重要です。

Watching the News

3. Understanding Check 1

　実際にニュースの中身を詳しく見ていく前に、どんな意見が交わされているのかを確認します。ここで具体的にニュースのイメージをつかむことが大事です。全体像を簡単にでも把握することで、ニュース理解の大きな助けとなります。

4. Understanding Check 2

　ニュースに関する問題を解くことで、どれだけニュースを理解できたか確認することができます。間違えた箇所に関しては、なぜ間違えたのかをしっかりと分析し、内容を正確に把握しましょう。Filling Gapsのアクティビティを行ってからUnderstanding Check 2に取り組むのも効果的かもしれません。

5. Filling Gaps
　ニュースの中で重要な意味を持つ単語を聞き取ります。何度も繰り返し聞き、正しい発音を意識します。それと同時に、単語を正しく書き取ることで、耳と手との両方の動きを通して重要単語を習得することを目指します。もし時間に余裕があれば、穴埋めの単語を実際に発音し、耳と手に加え口も使って覚えると効果的です。

Moving On
6. Making a Summary
　この箇所は、これまで観てきたニュースをまとめる部分でもあり、かつFollow Upに至る前の準備の段階でもあります。しっかりと内容を理解しているか、このアクティビティを通して確認しましょう。また、Building Languageで出てきた単語を再度使っているため、単語の習熟の確認ができるようになっています。

7. Follow Up
　ニュースと関連したトピックをいくつか挙げてあります。ニュースで得た知識、また単語を活かして話し合いを行うためのセクションです。トピックには、その場で話し合えるものと各自調べてから発表し合うもの、両方が含まれています。そのニュースに関してだけでなく、今後似たような話題に接したときにも意見を述べることができるよう、このアクティビティで仕上げを行います。

Background Information
　ニュースでは、必ずしもすべての事柄が説明されているとは限りません。ニュースの核となる事柄で、かつニュースの中ではあまり詳しく説明されていないことに関して、このセクションでは補足しています。ニュースをより深く理解するのにも役立ちますし、Follow Upでの話し合いの際にも使えるかもしれません。

Behind the Scenes
　ニュースに関連することではありますが、Background Informationとは異なりここではニュースの核となることではなく、話題が広がる知識、教養が深まる知識を取り上げました。肩の力を抜き、楽しんで読めるような内容になっています。

- テキスト添付のDVDには、各ユニットで取り上げたニュース映像が収録されています。
- テキスト準拠のAudio CDには、各ユニットのニュース音声と、ニュースを学習用に聞き取りやすく吹き替えた音声、Making a Summaryを収録しています。

Contents

Unit 1	Pie and Mash Shop Given Special Status — 1
	下町の老舗食堂、英国遺産に ［2分06秒］

Unit 2	Canterbury Girls' Choir — 7
	カンタベリー大聖堂に少女聖歌隊が誕生 ［2分32秒］

Unit 3	Festival for Geeks — 13
	ITオタクの祭典 ［2分11秒］

Unit 4	English Students Falling Behind in Maths — 19
	イングランドの中学生は数学が苦手？ ［2分45秒］

Unit 5	Saving the Elephants — 25
	象牙を求める密猟者から象を守る ［3分19秒］

Unit 6	Renovation of King's Cross Station — 31
	汚名返上？―生まれ変わったキングス・クロス駅 ［3分07秒］

Unit 7	Horse Therapy — 37
	馬との触れ合いでトラウマ克服へ ［2分37秒］

Unit 8   Cyber Monday ——————————————————— 43
「サイバー・マンデー」がやってきた ［3分14秒］

Unit 9   The Red Cross to Aid Food Poverty ———————— 49
食料難を解決しよう！ ［2分16秒］

Unit 10 Bike Hire Scheme ———————————————— 55
公共自転車レンタルシステムの未来 ［2分26秒］

Unit 11 Processed Meat Linked to Early Death ——————— 61
加工肉の食べ過ぎで早死にする危険が ［2分40秒］

Unit 12 Nursery Ratios Changed to Cut Fees ——————— 67
保育費削減で変わる？ イギリスの子育て事情 ［2分51秒］

Unit 13 Hope for the Blind ———————————————— 73
視力の再生を目指して ［2分38秒］

Unit 14 Being British —————————————————— 79
「イギリス人」それとも「イングランド人」？ ［2分57秒］

Unit 15 A New Gateway for Immigrants? ———————————— 85
自由を求めて海を渡る不法移民たち ［2分53秒］

Map of The United Kingdom

正式名称は **The United Kingdom of Great Britain and Northern Ireland**（グレートブリテン及び北アイルランド連合王国）。**England**（イングランド）、**Wales**（ウェールズ）、**Scotland**（スコットランド）、**Northern Ireland**（北アイルランド）の4国から成る連合国家です。

※（ ）は本テキストでその地名が登場するユニットを表します

Unit 1
Pie and Mash Shop Given Special Status

この度、ロンドンの下町にあるウナギとパイの店が保存指定建造物リストに記載されることになりました。その料理と建物にはどんな特徴があるのでしょうか。

▶ Starting Off

1 Setting the Scene

What do you think?

1. What do you think are good examples of traditional British food? Have you tried any?
2. What are some good examples of traditional Japanese food?
3. Have you ever been served some food that you found strange?

2 Building Language

Which word (1-5) best fits which explanation (a-e)?

1. evocative [ ]   a. main or important element
2. status   [ ]   b. rank or social standing
3. preserve [ ]   c. change character or composition
4. staple   [ ]   d. maintain in its original condition
5. alter   [ ]   e. bringing strong feelings or memories to mind

1

Watching the News

3 Understanding Check 1

Read the quotes, then watch the DVD and match them to the right people.

1. It's good old-fashioned Anglo-Saxon nosh. You can't beat it. [ ]

2. It's a unique piece of London's architectural history. [ ]

3. It's about as traditional as you get. It really is the best. [ ]

4. ... just one of the many reasons it's been listed. [ ]

4 Understanding Check 2

Which is the best answer?

1. When was L. Manze Eel, Pie and Mash Shop built?
   a. in the 1900s
   b. in the 1910s
   c. in the 1920s
   d. in the 1930s

2. How long has the current owner been at the shop?
   a. since the 1990s
   b. since the 1980s
   c. since the 1970s
   d. since the 1960s

3. Which of the following is NOT true?
   a. An eel pie and mash shop in east London has been given listed status.
   b. Pie and mash shops are very common in London.
   c. Listed buildings are protected by law.
   d. Pie and mash shops were a staple of early 20th century working-class life.

What do you remember?

4. What are some traditional features of pie and mash shops described in the news clip?

   ___

5. What does it mean to have listed status?

   ___

6. What are some of the reasons L. Manze Eel, Pie and Mash Shop has been given listed status?

   ___

●●Background Information●●

　今回L・マンジー店は、イングリッシュ・ヘリッジにより保存指定建造物2級に指定されました。同じく2級の建物にはビートルズがレコーディングを行った「アビー・ロード・スタジオ」などがあります。最初にロンドンに作られたウナギとパイの店は1844年のものだと言われており、1874年までには33軒、20世紀半ばまでには100軒と順調に数を増やしていました。

　この店がロンドン、そしてイングランドにとって重要な建築物であることは言うまでもありませんが、さらに大事なのは、この伝統的な建物をこれまで支えてきた料理です。ウナギ、パイ、マッシュポテトが名物とのことですが、一体どのような形で出され、どんな歴史があるのでしょうか。

　日本人にとってウナギ料理といえば蒲焼ですが、イースト・ロンドンではウナギをゼリー寄せにするかシチューに入れて食べるのが一般的でした。以前はテムズ川でもウナギがとれたため、新鮮な状態でウナギを調理して提供することが可能だったのです。栄養価も高く、労働者にとっては貴重な料理でした。

　パイとマッシュポテトという組み合わせはシンプルで、そのため安く売ることが可能でした。パイにウナギが入っていることもありますが、一般的には肉が入っており、労働者の力の源だったのです。労働者の体にもそして懐にもやさしいこの料理、現在ではあまり一般的ではなくなったとはいえ、L・マンジー店には時に有名人までもが訪れこの料理を楽しんでいくことがあるそうです。

　ニュース映像では、パイとマッシュポテトの乗った皿の上に、緑のソースがかけられています。これは「リカー」(liquor)と呼ばれ、バターや小麦粉、水、その他調味料の他にパセリの入ったソースです。これをたっぷりとかけて食べるのが、正しい楽しみ方です。

　1920年代からずっと変わらない建物がイースト・ロンドンに住む人々に大事にされてきたように、店のメニューも当時から変わらずロンドンっ子に愛され、彼らの胃袋を支えてきたのです。

参考：http://www.dailymail.co.uk/news/article-2480460/Pie-mash-shop-L-Manze-opened-1929-given-Grade-II-listing.html
http://www.english-heritage.org.uk/about/news/abbey-road-studios-grade-ii/
http://list.english-heritage.org.uk/resultsingle.aspx?uid=1416834

5 Filling Gaps

CD1-02 [Original]   CD1-03 [Voiced]

Watch the DVD, then fill the gaps in the text.

Newsreader: It's as London as black cabs and Beefeaters and now the L. Manze shop in Walthamstow has been (¹   ) Grade II listed (²   ) by English Heritage. As Helen Drew found out, they've been (³   ) (⁴   ) pie, mash and jellied eels since the twenties.

Helen Drew: Walthamstow High Street has a lot going on but you wouldn't (⁵   ) expect this – a pie and mash shop that's just been given listed status.

Drew: Built in the 1920s, L. Manze Eel, Pie and Mash Shop has been incredibly (⁶   ) (⁷   ), just one of the many reasons it's been listed. Traditional features include the white-tiled walls, mirrors and private booths.

Ed Vaizey MP, Culture Minister: It's a unique piece of London's architectural history. There've been eel and pie shops in our capital city for more than a hundred years and what we've got here is an (⁸   ) that hasn't really been (⁹   ) since the late 1920s.

Drew: The current owner has been here since the 1980s.

Jacqueline Cooper, Shop Owner: We have quite a few (¹⁰   ) customers. Our eldest one, brother and sister – she's 96 and he's 85 and they come in three times a week, maybe sometimes four.

Drew: Today's customers were certainly happy.

Customer 1: It's good old-fashioned Anglo-Saxon nosh. You can't beat it.

Customer 2: It's about as traditional as you get. It really is the best. I (¹¹   ) here, every week that I can, when I get my day off, purely for it, 'cos it's probably the best pie and mash in London.

Drew: How far do you come?

Customer 2: Er, I've come from Southend.

Drew: The shop is also a good example of a (^{12}) of early 20th century (^{13}) life.

Roger Bowdler, English Heritage: It's an amazing (^{14}) of once quite a common sort of (^{15}) in London: the pie and mash shop. And it's just so (^{16}). It's got all its atmosphere: all the fittings, all the booths, marble tops. It's just so (^{17}) of a whole way of (^{18}).

Drew: Listed status protects a building against unauthorized (^{19}) or (^{20}), but there are no changes planned here, especially not to the menu! Helen Drew, BBC London News.

(Wednesday 30 October 2013)

Notes ······

l. 2: **Beefeaters**「ロンドン塔の守衛」 l. 3: **Walthamstow**「ウォルサムストー」大ロンドンの一部でイースト・ロンドン郊外の地区 l. 4: **Grade II listed**「保存指定建造物2級リストに記載された」 l. 5: **English Heritage**「イングリッシュ・ヘリテッジ」イングランドの歴史的建造物、記念物を保存維持するために英国政府により設立された組織 l. 8: **jellied eels**「ウナギのゼリー寄せ」ロンドンの下町イーストエンドの名物。ぶつ切りにしたウナギを煮込んでから冷やしてゼリー状に固めたもの l. 14: **private booths**「ボックス席」 l. 21: **Our eldest one** 本来ならonesとなるはず。ones＝customers l. 24: **Anglo-Saxon**「アングロ・サクソン人の」5世紀頃、現在の北ドイツからブリテン島に移住した民族 l. 24: **nosh**「食事、軽食」 l. 31: **Southend**「サウスエンド」イングランド南東部の海港都市。正式名称はSouthend-on-Sea「サウスエンド・オン・シー」 l. 40: **marble tops**「大理石張りの表面」ここでは「店内の大理石張りのカウンター」のこと

Behind the Scenes

イギリスの魚料理

　今回のニュースで「ウナギのゼリー寄せ」が登場しましたが、イギリスでポピュラーな魚料理を挙げてみます。最も有名なのは、フィッシュ・アンド・チップス（fish and chips）で、白身魚（主にタラ〈cod〉ですが、乱獲により捕獲量が減り、価格が高騰し、最近では他のタラ科の魚〈pollackやhake〉で代用することがあるようです）とポテトのフライに塩やヴィネガーをかけて食べます。他には、フィッシュ・パイ（fish pie＝白身魚をホワイトソースでからめ、パイ皮の代わりにマッシュポテトで覆って、焼いたもの）、フィッシュ・ケーキ（fish cake＝魚のすり身で作った円盤型のコロッケ）があります。朝食にはキッパー（kipper＝ニシン〈herring〉の燻製）、子供たちに人気のフィッシュ・フィンガーズ（fish fingers＝長方形の魚のフライ）もあります。海に囲まれたイギリスですが、最近では魚の消費量は減っているようです。

▶▶▶ Moving On

6 Making a Summary　　　　　　　　　　　　　　　　　CD1-04

Fill the gaps to complete the summary.

　　An eel, pie and mash shop in east London has been awarded Grade II listed (s　　　　), which prevents any structural (a　　　　　　) being made without official (a　　　　　　). The L. Manze Shop was built in the 1920s, and many of its original features, such as white-tiled walls, mirrors and private (b　　　　　　), have been (p　　　　　　). It is (e　　　　　　) of early 20th century London, when eel, pie and mash shops were once a (s　　　　　　) of working-class life. It has many regular customers, some of whom travel from far away. A representative from the English Heritage organization thinks it is an amazing survival of a once common eatery.

7 Follow Up

Discuss, write or present.

1. Have you been to any restaurants that evoke memories of traditional life in that area?
2. What is the most interesting heritage site you have visited? Which heritage site would you most like to visit?
3. What kind of food was common in Japan at the beginning of the 20th century?

Unit 2
Canterbury Girls' Choir

カンタベリー大聖堂で少女聖歌隊が誕生しました。初めての公の場でのパフォーマンスを控えて、彼女たちはどんな気持ちでいるのでしょうか。また、少女聖歌の存在は教会音楽、ひいては教会にどんな影響を与えるのでしょう。

▶ Starting Off

1 Setting the Scene

What do you think?

1. What kind of music do you like?
2. Do you think that singing in a choir or chorus would be fun, or would it be hard work?
3. Do you think that girls and boys should always have the same opportunities? Can you think of any exceptions?

2 Building Language

Which word or phrase (1-5) best fits which explanation (a-e)?

1. pressure   [   ]   a. a great achievement
2. high expectations   [   ]   b. stress caused by a situation or by feeling forced to act in a certain way
3. commitment   [   ]   c. something that is your job or duty to deal with
4. responsibility   [   ]   d. a promise or firm decision to do something
5. no mean feat   [   ]   e. the feeling that someone is going to achieve a lot

▶▶ Watching the News

3 Understanding Check 1

Watch the DVD and choose T (true) or F (false) for each question.

1. This is the first girls' choir at Canterbury Cathedral.
   [T / F]

2. The girls are relaxed about it and think it is going to be easy.
   [T / F]

3. The choir director was surprised to find that the girls sang very well.
   [T / F]

4. The girls' choir sounds different from the male choir.
   [T / F]

4 Understanding Check 2

Which is the best answer?

1. How long have the girls been singing together? / When is their first public performance?
   a. since November / in two days
   b. for 900 years / next November
   c. for two days / the next weekend
   d. since this weekend / in November

2. What happened nearly 1,000 years ago? / What happened 20 years ago?
   a. The girls' choir stopped singing. / There were no more women priests.
   b. Canterbury Cathedral was built. / The girls' choir began.
   c. Choral music began at the Cathedral. / The first female priests were introduced.
   d. Women priests were introduced. / The male choir began.

3. Which of these sentences best describes the Cathedral choirs?
   a. The girls sing better than the males, but the males have more responsibilities.
   b. The males are under more pressure, but the girls have greater commitment.
   c. The girls have to work harder than the males, and are under more pressure.
   d. The girls don't sing as often as the males, but they have lots of responsibilities.

What do you remember?

4. How do the girls feel about their first public performance?

___

5. What does the Dean think about having both males and females in the choir?

___

6. How does the choir director see the future of the girls' choir?

___

●●Background Information●●

　英国国教会の総本山であるカンタベリー大聖堂では、これまで聖歌隊は男性によって構成されていましたが、今回初めて、(少女だけから成る)少女聖歌隊が誕生しました。ソールズベリー大聖堂においては、すでに20年も前から、そしてウィンチェスター大聖堂でも1998年に少女聖歌隊が結成されていて、ようやくカンタベリー大聖堂においても伝統を変える新しい動きが起こりました。イングランド全土では、少年聖歌隊員が1008名であるのに対し、少女聖歌隊員も765名にまで増えています。

　少女聖歌隊を結成することになった背景には、①聖歌隊で歌うことに興味を示す少年たちが減ってしまったこと②少女の場合、(声が)成熟するのが少年に比べて遅いため、聖歌隊への参加が年齢が上がってからでも可能であること③少女の場合、声変わりの心配がないこと④大聖堂で崇高な音楽に触れ、聖歌隊で歌うことは、少女たちにとっても教育上良いと考えられることが挙げられます。

　これに対して、①伝統を守りたい②少年の鋭く物悲しげな高音の声は、少女の声では出せない③(少女聖歌隊は)新たに費用がかかる④新たに指導しなければならないという理由から、少女聖歌隊に反対する人たちもいます。

　伝統を守ることを強く主張する団体(Campaign for the Traditional Cathedral Choirなど)は、男性のみによって構成される聖歌隊が存続することに価値を置き、少年聖歌隊と少女聖歌隊が一緒に歌うことも快く思っていません。しかし、ウィンチェスター大聖堂では、イースターやクリスマスに少年聖歌隊と少女聖歌隊が一緒に歌うこともあるようですが、抗議を受けたことはないと言います。

　現在、少女聖歌隊は、少年聖歌隊が学校休暇の間に代わりに歌うのみですが、今後はますます活躍の場が広がるかもしれません。

参考：http://www.telegraph.co.uk/culture/music/classicalmusic/10588016/The-history-girls-Canterbury-Cathedrals-first-girls-choir.html

http://www.huffingtonpost.com/2014/01/15/canterbury-cathedral-girls-choir_n_4597726.html

5 Filling Gaps

CD1-05 [Original] CD1-06 [Voiced]

Watch the DVD, then fill the gaps in the text.

Newsreader: And finally, for 900 years the choir at Canterbury Cathedral has been (¹   ) (²   ), but this weekend, history will be made. Here's John Maguire.

John Maguire: They've only been together since November. But, just listen to this.

Maguire: The girls are just two days away from their first (³   ) (⁴   ) in Canterbury Cathedral. Two days away from making history.

Girl 1: I think this is a really good opportunity in a really special choir. I think that's why it's scarier than . . .

Girl 2: It's quite a lot of (⁵   ) being the first girls' choir.

Girl 3: It's quite (⁶   ) (⁷   ) for us.

Girl 2: To prove ourselves as girl choristers, the first time is gonna be . . . it's gonna be really exciting, but quite a lot of (⁸   ) probably.

Maguire: Now, the male choir has to sing every day. The girls won't quite have that level of (⁹   ), but if they're in any doubt about the (¹⁰   ) they're about to take on, just look at this. Already, they're (¹¹   ) (¹²   ) by the international media and that's before singing a note in public.

Maguire: It's only 20 years since the first women priests in the Church of England, and so far, no (¹³   ) bishops. So, are girls' voices in the choir stalls long overdue?

The Very Reverend Dr Robert Willis, Dean of Canterbury: I think that the sound that we're (¹⁴   ) with the boys and with this, this older, um, choir of girls, they'll be different sounds. I've no doubt that, that in the future there will be times when they all sing together. But one can achieve a

10

(^{15}) of musical sounds, which we, we've heard, eh, already developing.

Maguire: Recruited from local schools, the girls have only met a few times, but their director David Newsholme believes they've made (^{16}) (^{17}).

David Newsholme, Choir Director: Er, it was no surprise to find that they sang very well together indeed, and, um, and hopefully take on a little bit more in the Cathedral and, and possibly away from the Cathedral. From the odd (^{18}), going on the occasional (^{19}), and possibly even making a (^{20}) in the future. Who knows?

Maguire: Musically, this girls' choir will (^{21}) a new sound for Canterbury Cathedral, when this particular group makes history. (^{22}) (^{23}) (^{24}) when you consider choral music here dates back almost 1,000 years. John Maguire, BBC News, Canterbury.

(Thursday 23 January 2014)

Notes

l. 7: **just**「ともかく」命令文とともに、注意を引く際に用いられる　l. 15: **prove ourselves**「私たちに実力があることを証明する」　l. 15: **choristers**「聖歌隊員」　l. 17: **won't quite** "not quite"は部分否定。「必ずしも～というわけではない」　l. 19: **take on**「（責任）を負う」　l. 21: **singing a note**「歌声を披露する」noteは音符の意味　l. 22: **the Church of England**「英国国教会」正確には英国（イギリス）全体の教会ではなくイングランドの教会だが、日本語の訳語としては「英国国教会」が使われることが多い　l. 23: **choir stalls**「聖歌隊席」　l. 27: **older**「（少年たちより）年上の」聖歌隊を構成するメンバーは男の子が8–13歳、女の子が12–16歳　l. 42: **odd**「時たまの、時折の」　l. 46: **, when ...** 関係副詞の非制限用法　l. 46: **particular** 文脈で特定されたものを指して、「その」「この」の意味を強める。何を指示しているのかを明らかにする役割であり、訳さなくてよい場合が多い

Behind the Scenes

巡礼の地カンタベリー

601年に修道士アウグスティヌスが初代カンタベリー大司教に就任して以来、カンタベリーは常にイングランドのキリスト教の中心にありました。1170年には、ヘンリー2世と対立したカンタベリー大司教トマス・ベケットが大聖堂内の祭壇で暗殺されました。その後、ベケットは殉教者として列聖され、多くの巡礼者たちがカンタベリーを訪れるようになりました。この「カンタベリー詣で」を枠組みに、ジェフリー・チョーサー（Geoffrey Chaucer, c.1343-1400）が『カンタベリー物語』(*The Canterbury Tales*, 1387?-1400) を著しました。1534年、ヘンリー8世の離婚問題でイングランドの教会がカトリックのローマ教会から分離し、英国国教会が国教となると、カンタベリーはその総本山となり、現在まで揺るぎない地位を誇っています。

▶▶▶ Moving On

6 Making a Summary

CD1-07

Fill the gaps to complete the summary.

Last November, the first girls' choir at Canterbury Cathedral was formed, and they were soon going to give their first public (p   ). This was (n   ) (m   ) (f   ) because for nearly 1,000 years, the choir had been male only. The girls thought it was a good (o   ), but felt a lot of (p   ) and knew that there were (h   ) (e   ), so they were finding the experience (s   ). They had less time (c   ) than the male choir, but were still taking on a lot of (r   ), because of the interest from international media. The Dean thought it was good to mix boys' and girls' voices because they could achieve a (d   ) of musical sounds. The choir director thought the girls sang very well, and thought they might even tour and make recordings.

7 Follow Up

Discuss, write or present.

1. Do you think it is strange that there were no females in the choir for so long? Can you think of any similar situations in Japan?
2. Why do you think the girls found being in the choir scary? Would you feel the same in a similar situation?
3. Do you prefer songs to be sung by men only or females only, or do you prefer the voices to be mixed? Can you think of some examples?

Unit 3
Festival for Geeks

何千人もの若者がロンドン郊外のグリニッジのイベント会場に集まっています。一体何が行われているのでしょうか。

▶ Starting Off

1 Setting the Scene

What do you think?

1. Are you an enthusiast of new technology? How good are you at using computers?
2. What technological inventions have influenced your life the most?
3. Do you play video games? What is your favourite video game?

2 Building Language

Which word (1-5) best fits which explanation (a-e)?

1. extravaganza [ ]   a. make generally available
2. epicentre   [ ]   b. occurring every year
3. innovation   [ ]   c. new method or idea
4. release   [ ]   d. spectacular entertainment display
5. annual   [ ]   e. central point

13

Watching the News

3 Understanding Check 1

Read the quotes, then watch the DVD and match them to the right people.

1. It puts us back on the map again in technology world. [ ]

2. ... more and more people are coming to London ... [ ]

3. We're great with technology in Britain. We, we're fantastic at gaming. [ ]

4. Well, this being Glastonbury for geeks, where else would you expect to sleep ... [ ]

4 Understanding Check 2

Which is the best answer?

1. Where will Campus Party take place?
   a. The O2
   b. Spain
   c. Glastonbury
   d. Wembley Stadium

2. What age group is targeted by Campus Party?
   a. under 12
   b. 20s
   c. 18 to 30s
   d. over 65s

3. What are many people excited about seeing?
   a. the new PlayStation
   b. the new Xbox One
   c. the new iPhone
   d. the new Galaxy tablet

What do you remember?

4. Where will lots of people who join the event be staying?

　

5. How long will the event last?

　

6. Where have the 200 electronic engineering students come from?

　

●●Background Information●●

　キャンパス・パーティーは「ITオタク」の若者が世界中から集まるイベントです。ここに集まる人々はコンピューターのハッカーや開発業者、ゲーマーなど、職業は多岐にわたりますが、みなテクノロジーの愛好家、言い換えれば「ITオタク」であることは共通しています。

　2013年ロンドン大会の開催中は24時間イベントが行われており、参加者は休む暇なくこのイベントを楽しみました。会場では、会議やディベートを行ったり、ワークショップを行ったり、講演を聞いたりと、様々なイベントに参加します。また、コンサートや映画などの娯楽も用意されており飽きることはありません。賞金の出るゲーム大会もあります。歩いて数分のところにあるロンドン・サッカー・ドームは参加者が寝泊まりできる場所として提供されています。また、食事は24時間提供されており、ベジタリアンや宗教的な制約がある参加者への配慮もなされています。

　キャンパス・パーティーが最初に行われたのは1997年です。スペインで行われ、その後はスペイン語圏、または南米での開催が続いていました（メキシコ、コロンビア、ポルトガルなど）が、最近ではベルリンでも2012年に開催されています。はじめは250人しか参加者がいませんでしたが、16年の間に活動はグローバルになり、今ではキャンパス・パーティーのコミュニティには26万4千人ものメンバーがいて、このイベントを楽しみにしています。

　2013年のこのイベントは「オタクたちにとってのグラストンベリー・フェスティバル（イギリス最大の音楽フェス）」であると言われました。このイベントに例えられたことで、キャンパス・パーティーの知名度は今後ますます上がっていくかもしれません。

5 Filling Gaps

CD1-08 [Original] CD1-09 [Voiced]

Watch the DVD, then fill the gaps in the text.

Newsreader: Next, thousands of people camping in tents, (¹   ) (²   ) their smartphones and laptops, and it's all happening at The O2 in Greenwich. But they're not (³   ) in line for tickets to a big music concert. They're here for one of the biggest technology events in the world, which has come to London for the first time. Alice Bhandhukravi has been finding out more.

Alice Bhandhukravi: It's a seven-day (⁴   ) targeted at the 18 to 30s but this is not just another festival. This is Campus Party, for people who love (⁵   ). In fact, they love it so much, they've travelled all over the world to be here. Well, this being Glastonbury for geeks, where else would you expect to sleep other than a tent with three and a half thousand other (⁶   )?

Participant 1: We've gone, er, 200 people. We've come from (⁷   ) and we are here because we are students of engineering, electronic engineering.

Participant 2: It puts us back on the map again in technology world. You know, rather than going (⁸   ) to Campus Party, or any other technology event, we're actually going back home.

Bhandhukravi: So, it's all fun and gaming here with a bit of (⁹   ) and (¹⁰   ) to boot. But it's also about making the most of (¹¹   ) (¹²   ) for people with the right skills, and the (¹³   ), so we're told, is the place to be.

Ronan Dunne, Chief Executive, O2 UK: London is now the (¹⁴   ) for technology and (¹⁵   ), not just in the UK but in Europe, and more and more people are coming to London, whether it be at Tech City or elsewhere, to find the great (¹⁶   ) that are in the market here.

Bhandhukravi: And it's also a great opportunity to see this. Now, this is kind

16

of a big deal. And for many of the gamers here, this will be the (^{17}) of their week because this is the brand new Xbox, Xbox One, which hasn't even been (^{18}) yet.

Suzi Perry, presenter: We're great with technology in Britain. We, we're fantastic at gaming. We've got some really good people, some innovations, and we should try and get them to come here on an, on an, (^{19}) basis. And this is a, this is a, perfect (^{20}) for it. Why not?

Bhandhukravi: So, for the digitally minded, this corner of Greenwich promises to be a lot of fun. Alice Bhandhukravi, BBC London News.

(Monday 2 September 2013)

Notes

l. 4: **The O2** グリニッジにある大規模娯楽施設。旧名称はミレニアム・ドーム。O2はスポンサーであるイギリスの携帯電話会社　l. 5: **Greenwich**「グリニッジ」大ロンドン南東部の町。テムズ川の南岸に位置する　l. 11: **Campus Party**「キャンパス・パーティー」1997年から毎年開催されるITイベント。2013年度は9月2日から7日にかけて行われた　l. 13: **Glastonbury**「グラストンベリー」イングランド南西部サマセットの町。1970年から大規模野外ロック・フェスティバルが開催されている　l. 18: **It puts us back on the map again**「このイベントにより、イギリスは再び有名になる」　l. 22: **to boot**「おまけに」　l. 28: **Tech City**「テック・シティ」イースト・ロンドンに位置し、ロンドンのシリコンバレーと呼ばれるIT産業の盛んな地域　l. 36: **Xbox One** マイクロソフト社が開発した家庭用ゲーム機。イギリスでは2013年11月22日に発売された　l. 43: **the digitally minded**「デジタル式の考え方をする人々」

Behind the Scenes

「経度0度を示す」グリニッジ子午線

　グリニッジは、元来、経度0度を表す「グリニッジ子午線」(Prime Meridian at Greenwich)が通るグリニッジ天文台(Royal Greenwich Observatory)のある場所として有名です。かつては太陽の運行をもとに各国がそれぞれに一日の始まりと終わりを設定し、多数の本初子午線が存在していましたが、グリニッジ子午線が基準となってからは、世界全体で共通の時間を刻むようになりました。残念ながら、現在国際的に使用されている本初子午線は、グリニッジ子午線から東に5.64秒、102.5 mのところにあるIERS基準子午線(IERS Reference Meridian, GPSなどに使われるアメリカが構築した基準)に変わってしまいました。しかし、グリニッジ天文台(の敷地内)に南北に描かれた経度0度を示す白い線をまたいで記念写真を撮る観光客も多く、ここが人気の観光名所であることに変わりはありません。

▶▶▶ Moving On

6 Making a Summary

CD1-10

Fill the gaps to complete the summary.

　　　Thousands of people from all over the world are coming to The O2 in Greenwich for an event. It is the first time the (a　　　　　) event has ever taken place in London. It's a seven-day technology (e　　　　　) called Campus Party, for people who love technology. There will be lots of hacking, coding, and chances to play new computer games, but it is also about looking for job (o　　　　　). London is now the (e　　　　) for technology and (i　　　　　) in Europe, and many people are coming to London to find the great innovators that are in the market here. Many gamers are especially excited about the chance to see the new Xbox One, which hasn't even been (r　　　　) yet.

7 Follow Up

Discuss, write or present.

1. Are you aware of any 'cutting edge' research taking place right now?
2. What do you think will be the next great technological breakthrough?
3. Does technology always improve society? Can you think of examples of how technology has changed society for the better, or for the worse?

Unit 4
English Students Falling Behind in Maths

アジアの国々に迫る勢いで、優秀な算数の成績をおさめているイングランドの小学生。しかし成長するにつれ、その能力は伸び悩むことがわかりました。

▶ Starting Off

1 Setting the Scene

What do you think?

1. Which do you think is the most important school subject, and why?
2. Why do you think that some pupils do worse than others on maths tests? Is it just because they are not good at maths, or are there other reasons?
3. Do you think Japanese pupils are better or worse at maths than pupils in other countries?

2 Building Language

For each word (1-5), find two synonyms (a-j).

1. counterpart [/   ]
2. core   [/   ]
3. consistent   [/   ]
4. leapfrog   [/   ]
5. stretch   [/   ]

a. opposite number
b. unfailing
c. advance quickly
d. challenge
e. regular
f. overtake
g. essential
h. test
i. corresponding person
j. central

▶▶ Watching the News

3 Understanding Check 1

Read the quotes, then watch the DVD and match them to the right people.

1. In other words it could be, say, pushy parents, or it could be other cultural factors that's driving this. [ ]

2. It's good to be good at maths ... [ ]

3. The study also found that Scottish students overtake those in England by the time they're 16. [ ]

4. ... unfortunately there are a lot of distractions for our students. [ ]

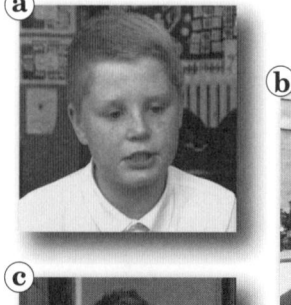

4 Understanding Check 2

Which is the best answer?

1. Which three countries are consistently top of international school tables?
   a. England, Japan, Hong Kong
   b. Singapore, Japan, China
   c. Singapore, Hong Kong, Taiwan
   d. China, Japan, Scotland

2. Where do the maths scores of English 10-year-old students rank?
   a. fifth
   b. ninth
   c. third
   d. eighth

3. What other differences between education in England and Asia are mentioned in the report?
   a. brighter students and better schools
   b. widespread private tutoring and higher teacher salaries
   c. fewer distractions and smaller classes
   d. stricter teachers and longer schooldays

What do you remember?

4. What are the names of the tests taken by primary and GCSE pupils?

   _____

5. According to the secondary school teacher, why are students in England falling behind?

   _____

6. What factors outside the schooling system might be driving these results?

   _____

●●Background Information●●

　経済協力開発機構（OECD）が世界65カ国の15歳を対象に、3年ごとに行っている国際学力到達度調査（PISA）で、イギリスの子どもたちは数学において、世界（特にアジア）の国々よりも大きく遅れていることが分かりました。この結果は、10歳児を対象に行われた国際数学・理科教育調査（TIMSS）の結果と併せて考えると、11歳以降の教育、すなわち、中等教育の在り方について、さらなる見直しを促すものとなりそうです。

　中等学校での学力低下は、①クラス内の中間層に学習内容のレベルが合わせられてしまい、優秀な生徒の学力が十分に伸ばされないこと②学習内容が、相互に関連性のない個別の事柄をただ暗記し、反復練習することに留まり、より複雑な問題を解決する能力が育まれないこと③一年早くGCSE（義務教育修了の際に行う統一試験）を受験させられるため、必要な学習内容を十分に習得できていないことによると考えられます。これらの背景には、学校の評価に関わる学校別成績一覧が「GCSEで（5科目において）C以上の成績を取った生徒の割合」を主な指標としているため、少しでもその数を増やそうとする学校の事情があるようです（Aを取る必要はないので、C以上を取らせることに教育の標準が合わせられたり、優秀な生徒に一年早い受験をさせ、翌年は〈残りの〉他科目の勉強に集中させて確実に5科目でのC以上を取らせるようにすることもあります※）。

　サッチャー政権下の1988年より、①「全国共通カリキュラム」と「全国テスト」が実施され、②「学校選択の自由」が保障され、続くメージャー政権下の1993年から③学校別成績一覧の公開が始まると、学校間の競争が激化しました。また、1992年創設の「教育水準監査局」（OFSTED）による学校監査、監査結果の公開も、学校に一層プレッシャーをかけることとなりました。

　政府は、2013年9月より（このPISAのランキング発表前の時点で）、GCSEの数学で「C」以上の成績を取れなかった生徒に対して、18歳まで数学を学ぶことを義務づけており、かねてより懸念されていた学力低下への取り組みを始めています。

　　※GCSEの受験方法（早期受験など）については、いろいろ問題が指摘され、変更が検討されています。

参考：http://www.bbc.com/news/uk-24326087
　　　http://www.telegraph.co.uk/education/educationnews/9279379/Ofsted-bright-children-failed-by-poor-maths-lessons.html

5 Filling Gaps

CD1-11 [Original] CD1-12 [Voiced]

Watch the DVD, then fill the gaps in the text.

Newsreader: The top maths students in England are two years (¹   ) those in Hong Kong and Taiwan by the time they sit their GCSEs. That's according to research from the University of London. It shows that they can match their foreign (²   ) at the age of 10, but then they start to fall behind. The study also found that Scottish students overtake those in England by the time they're 16. Our education correspondent, Reeta Chakrabarti, explains.

Teacher: Seven times tables, nice and loud. Off we go.

Reeta Chakrabarti: Maths is a (³   ) (⁴   ) and the brightest 10-year-olds in England are as good at it as their peers in most high performing countries. These primary pupils (⁵   ) how important it is.

Student 1: It's good to be good at maths because when you, you can find it in real life problems and if you didn't know how to do maths then you probably couldn't get on with a lot of things in life.

Student 2: I find it fun but sometimes I find it a bit hard.

Chakrabarti: Singapore, along with Hong Kong and Taiwan are (⁶   ) top of international school tables. Ten-year-olds in England do (⁷   ) as (⁸   ) as those in Hong Kong and Taiwan, but by 16 they fall behind. Today's research used two different international maths tests: one known as TIMSS, for primary school children, and the other PISA, taken by GCSE pupils. They show that in 2003, 10-year-olds in England came fifth behind the East Asian countries, with Scotland 11th. A separate study, in 2009, of 16-year-olds, shows England in ninth place, with Scotland (⁹   ) into seventh place. What is happening to young mathematicians in England? One maths teacher at a London secondary school says bright pupils just aren't (¹⁰   ) (¹¹   ).

Moses Kabba, maths teacher: Education in, ah, Asian countries is much more respected than it is here. Er, unfortunately there are a lot of distractions for our students. So, therefore they're not as, um, if you like, they're not driven as much as our Asian (^{12}). And especially in maths, the brighter students aren't (^{13}) as well as they should be ...

Chakrabarti: But there are other differences, such as (^{14}) private tutoring in East Asia and higher teacher salaries. And researchers say East Asian children who've been through the English system do very well at these tests too.

Dr John Jerrim, Institute of Education: It's things going on outside of the (^{15}) (^{16}), and particularly outside secondary schools, that's driving these results. In other words it could be, say, pushy parents, or it could be other cultural factors that's driving this.

Teacher: 145 plus ...

Chakrabarti: But (^{17}) (^{18}) is important to ministers who say their changes will mean these primary children will do better with tougher exams and improved teaching. The (^{19}) (^{20}) of the future will show if they're correct. Reeta Chakrabarti, BBC News.

(Friday 22 February 2013)

Notes ··

l. 1: **maths**「算数、数学」ここでは両方の意味で使われている。アメリカ英語ではmathが一般的 l. 4: **sit ~**「~（試験）を受ける」 l. 4: **GCSEs**「一般中等教育修了試験（General Certificate of Secondary Education）」イングランド、ウェールズ、北アイルランド（スコットランドは含まれない）では義務教育の修了時である16歳にこのテストを受験する。1986年に導入、1988年に初めてのテストが行われたシステムで、それまでのO(Ordinary)レベル試験とCSE（Certificate of Secondary Education＝中等教育修了試験）を統合したもの。大学入学に際してはA（Advanced）レベル試験を受ける必要がある l. 11: **Seven times tables**「（掛け算の）7の段の表」 l. 11: **nice and ~**「十分、とても~」後に来る形容詞を強調する役割を持つ l. 11: **Off we go.**「いきましょう。」 l. 24: **TIMSS**「国際数学・理科教育動向調査（Trends in International Mathematics and Science Study）」算数・数学、理科の力が試される。イギリスでは第4学年（8~9歳）、第8学年（12~13歳）の生徒に対して行われる l. 24: **PISA**「国際学習到達度調査（Programme for International Student Assessment）」15歳児を対象に読解力、数学的リテラシー、科学的リテラシーの力を測定 l. 34: **if you like**「~とも言えるでしょう」 l. 44: **It's things ... that's driving these results.** 強調構文。本来ならthat's drivingはthingsに対応しているのでthat are drivingになるところ

Unit 4 *English Students Falling Behind in Maths* 23

Behind the Scenes

『ハリー・ポッター』に見られる「Oレベル試験」

　GCSE「一般中等教育修了試験」は1988年以前、「Oレベル（O-level＝Ordinary Level）試験」と呼ばれていました。この「Oレベル試験」は『ハリー・ポッター』シリーズにO.W.L.（＝Ordinary Wizarding Level）Tests「普通魔法レベル試験」またの名を「ふくろうテスト」として登場します。物語の中で、ハリーたちは、第5学年の学年末にこの試験を受けることになり、呪文学や薬草学、魔法史などの学科を猛勉強します。ちなみに『ハリー・ポッター』には、N.E.W.T.（＝Nastily Exhausting Wizarding Tests）「めちゃくちゃ疲れる魔法試験・いもりテスト」というものも登場し、こちらは現実の「Aレベル（A-level＝Advanced Level）試験」になぞらえて創作されています。

▶▶▶ Moving On

6　Making a Summary

Fill the gaps to complete the summary.

　Maths is a (c　　　　) academic subject, and students understand its importance. Students in Singapore, Hong Kong and Taiwan in East Asia (c　　　　　　) perform very well on maths tests, and English primary school students perform almost as well, ranking fifth in the world, ahead of Scotland, which is ranked 11th. However, by the time they reach secondary school, English students fall behind their East Asian (c　　　　　　) into ninth place being (l　　　　　　) by Scotland. One secondary school teacher suggests that the brightest English students aren't being (s　　　　　) enough. Another suggestion is that (w　　　　) private tutoring and higher teacher salaries give East Asian students an advantage. Influences outside the schooling system, such as (p　　　　) parents and other cultural (f　　　　　) may also drive these results.

7　Follow Up

Discuss, write or present.

1. What do you think are the strengths and weaknesses of Japan's educational system?
2. Why do you think many East Asian countries consistently rank highly in their maths scores?
3. What academic subjects do you think Japanese students are traditionally strongest and weakest at? Can you think of any reasons for this?

Unit 5
Saving the Elephants

アフリカでは、象牙を求める密猟者によって多くの象が殺されています。象を守るために、どのような取り組みが行われているのでしょうか。

▶ Starting Off

1 Setting the Scene

What do you think?

1. Which animals are the most endangered in the world?
2. Is it legal to sell ivory in Japan? Are any other animal products illegal?
3. Is smuggling a big problem in Japan? What kinds of things are smuggled into Japan?

2 Building Language

Which word (1-5) best fits which explanation (a-e)?

1. unprecedented [ ]   a. area of land
2. vulnerable   [ ]   b. well-known
3. renowned   [ ]   c. never done or known before
4. territory   [ ]   d. very destructive or damaging
5. devastating   [ ]   e. weak and unsafe

25

▶▶ Watching the News

3 Understanding Check 1

Read the quotes, then watch the DVD and match them to the right people.

1. ... or a guy actually sits up the tree and spears the elephant from the top. [ ]

2. ... in this day and age it's an indictment on mankind. [ ]

3. They are not beating us. Our men are dealing with them effectively ... [ ]

(a)

(b)

(c)

4 Understanding Check 2

Which is the best answer?

1. According to the report, which country leads the ivory trade?
   a. China
   b. Kenya
   c. The USA
   d. The UK

2. What is the shocking statistic about the number of elephants killed by poachers?
   a. One elephant is killed every day.
   b. One elephant is killed every hour.
   c. One elephant is killed every 30 minutes.
   d. One elephant is killed every 15 minutes.

3. How many elephants are estimated to have been killed by poachers in 2012?
   a. 20,000
   b. 22,000
   c. 30,000
   d. 32,000

What do you remember?

4. What is Kenya doing to try and stop the ivory trade?

   _____

5. How many elephants remain in Kenya today?

   _____

6. What does Charles Musyoki, from Kenya Wildlife Service believe the census will indicate?

   _____

●●Background Information●●

　今回のニュースは、アフリカにおける象牙目当ての象の密猟問題についてでした。1970年代初頭、象牙の需要が高まると、象の密猟が横行し、象の個体数が大幅に減少しました。そこで、1989年にCITES (Convention on International Trade in Endangered Species of Wild Fauna and Flora)、いわゆる「ワシントン条約」が締結され、象牙の国際取引が禁止されました。1990年にこの条約が執行されると、象の密猟は激減し、ヨーロッパとアメリカの主な象牙市場は消滅しました。しかし、1999年には、ボツワナ、ナミビア、ジンバブエが49,000 kgの象牙を日本に販売することが許可され、2008年にも105,000 kgの象牙が日本と中国に向けて輸出されました。その後も、2009年には、世界で20,000 kgの象牙が押収され、2011年には、差押えの上位13件だけで23,000 kgの押収量になり、さらに2012年10月から2013年1月の12週間には、4件で12,000 kgの象牙が押収されるなど、象の密猟と象牙の違法取引は、近年悪化の一途をたどっています。

　象を絶滅から守るためには、CITESによる象牙取引の全面禁止を求める署名活動や象の保護を目的とした基金への寄付などが有効です。また、私たち消費者の意識を変え、象牙の需要を減らすことが必要であると思われます。

参考：http://www.bornfree.org.uk/animals/african-elephants/projects/ivory-trade/
　　　http://www.bloodyivory.org/stop-the-ivory-trade

5 Filling Gaps

CD1-14 [Original]   CD1-15 [Voiced]

Watch the DVD, then fill the gaps in the text.

Newsreader: Conservationists say the (¹   ) wildlife trade is reaching (²   ) levels. Across Africa it's estimated around 22,000 elephants were killed in 2012 by poachers for their ivory. Later this week the Prince of Wales and Prince William will (³   ) the Prime Minister in hosting an international conference aimed at (⁴   ) the problem. Our correspondent, Mark Lowen, has been to Tsavo National Park in Kenya to see how rangers are (⁵   ) back against the poachers.

Mark Lowen: Africa's (⁶   ) under threat, hunted by the poachers. Thirty years ago Kenya had almost 170,000 elephants. Today around 30,000 remain. A (⁷   ) ivory trade led by (⁸   ) has reached record levels. As dawn breaks over Tsavo National Park, a week-long aerial census begins to gauge the poaching impact. It's a vital tool for the rangers who believe they're (⁹   ) the fight.

Charles Musyoki, Kenya Wildlife Service: We're (¹⁰   ) beating the poachers. We are beating them. They are not beating us. Our men are dealing with them effectively and, the census will basically be an indicator of, that we've been (¹¹   ).

Lowen: The planes circled over the savannah.

Pilot: Five, six, seven, eight . . .

Lowen: Teams counting the elephants to see if new births are outweighing those poached. There is a (¹²   ) statistic in Africa that an elephant is killed by poachers every 15 minutes. The hope of this census is that it will show a resilient elephant population, but also indicate where they are and if they're straying into (¹³   ) too (¹⁴   ) to the poachers.

Lowen: But then the hard reality: our cameraman is allowed to join a small vet team that hears of a newly (¹⁵   ) elephant. It's a huge bull with prize tusks, hit by poachers for the fourth time. The gun saves him, an anaesthetic dart to give the team time to work.

Nick Trent, Conservation Manager: As he's walking under a tree, the, whatever's gone in, has gone in here like this, so it's likely a spear. So what a guy does is, he either sets an automatic spear up a tree with a (¹⁶   ) on it, that the elephant trips and the spear falls, or a guy actually sits up the tree and spears the elephant from the top.

Lowen: A special clay sucks out the (¹⁷   ) and heals the wounds. Two more weeks and he'd have been dead. He has to be pulled up, a new lease of life until the poachers strike again.

Lowen: So how old is this one, for example?

Dame Daphne Sheldrick, Founder, David Sheldrick Wildlife Trust: Tundani? He's, he's about what, three years old now, not quite.

Lowen: For one of the world's most (¹⁸   ) elephant experts, the extent of poaching is hard to (¹⁹   ).

Sheldrick: Terrible, really terrible. It's a … in this day and age it's an indictment on mankind. We're looking at about 10, 15 years before elephants in the wild disappear.

Lowen: China's (²⁰   ) for ivory kills here. Kenya is trying higher fines for smugglers. But saving this precious (²¹   ) is more critical than ever. Mark Lowen, BBC News in Kenya.

(Tuesday 11 February 2014)

Notes

l. 6: **Prince of Wales**「プリンス・オブ・ウェールズ」英国国王の法定推定継承人である長男に国王によって授けられる皇太子の称号。チャールズ皇太子（1948- ）のこと l. 7: **Prince William**「ウィリアム王子（1982- ）」チャールズ皇太子とダイアナ元妃の長男 l. 10: **Tsavo National Park**「ツァボ国立公園」ケニア南東部にある l. 15: **aerial census**「航空機からの調査」GPS機能を備えた航空機から動物の（今回は、象の）個体数を数える調査 l. 18: **Kenya Wildlife Service**「ケニア野生生物庁」 l. 27: **a resilient elephant population**「象の個体数の回復が早い［増えてきている］こと」 l. 31: **an anaesthetic dart**「麻酔薬のついた投げ矢」 l. 45: **David Sheldrick Wildlife Trust**「デイヴィッド・シェルドリック・ワイルドライフ・トラスト」ケニアにある野生動物保護団体。親を失い孤児となった象を保護し、野生復帰のための支援活動を行う l. 46: **what**「まあ、さあ」数量を表すのに言いよどむ時の表現 l. 49: **indictment on mankind**「人間に大きな非があること（を示しています）」

Behind the Scenes

象牙と植民地問題

イギリスの作家ジョゼフ・コンラッド (Joseph Conrad, 1857-1924) は『闇の奥』(*Heart of Darkness*, 1902) で、ベルギー領コンゴで商人クルツ (Kurtz) が象牙の売買をする様子を描いています。クルツは、権力を利用して象牙を手に入れ、ヨーロッパへと送っていたのです。教化、啓蒙という言葉を隠れ蓑に搾取を続けてきた先進国と、不当に搾取されながらもその不平等性を是正する声をあげることのできなかった途上国との複雑な関係が象牙に象徴されていると言えるでしょう。

しかしクルツは、その後身勝手な行動の報いを受けることとなります。アフリカの闇、そして自身の内なる闇に取り込まれたクルツは理性を失い、狂気のうちに命を落とします。搾取によるゆがんだ関係は、搾取する側にも価値観の転換を迫らずにはいないのです。

▶▶▶ Moving On

6 Making a Summary

CD1-16

Fill the gaps to complete the summary.

The illegal trade in ivory is reaching (u   ) levels, and the effect it is having on the elephant population of Africa is (d   ). It is estimated that (p   ) killed 22,000 elephants across Africa for their ivory in 2012, but The Kenyan Wildlife Service is fighting back. They hope a (c   ) in Tsavo National Park will indicate that they are beating the poachers, and help them understand where elephants live and if they are moving into (t   ) that makes them (v   ) to poaching. A (r   ) elephant expert is worried that elephants in the wild could (d   ) completely in the near future. Most ivory is sold in China, and the Kenyan government is imposing higher fines for (s   ).

7 Follow Up

Discuss, write or present.

1. Are you aware of any conservation projects taking place in Japan?
2. There is a very interesting conservation project called the Frozen Ark project (http://www.frozenark.org). Can you imagine from the name what this project is about?
3. Conservation groups sometimes criticise Japan for whaling. What do you think about the practice of whaling?

Unit 6
Renovation of King's Cross Station

長年、ロンドンのキングス・クロス駅周辺は、さびれた、いかがわしい地域でしたが、この度、駅が改築され、便利で活気ある地域へと生まれ変わりました。巨額の費用がかかったこの事業に対する人々の声を聞いてみましょう。

▶ Starting Off

1 Setting the Scene

What do you think?

1. Which train station(s) do you use regularly?
2. Are there any stations you particularly like or dislike? Why?

2 Building Language

Which word (1-5) best fits which explanation (a-e)?

1. associated   [ ]   a. use money to make a profit
2. regenerate   [ ]   b. a piece of outstanding workmanship
3. masterpiece [ ]   c. connected to something else
4. benefit   [ ]   d. renew, bring back to life
5. invest   [ ]   e. advantage gained

▶▶ Watching the News

3 Understanding Check 1

Read the quotes, then watch the DVD and match them to the right people.

1. ... a place to stay where you can wait for your friends, family, whoever. [ ]

2. The trains, the track, the signalling, that's obviously critical but people need to be able to circulate smoothly ... [ ]

3. ... behind me, there, you will see the beautiful facade – it hasn't been on show since the 1860s. [ ]

4. ... and I think the whole area is stunning. [ ]

4 Understanding Check 2

Which is the best answer?

1. When was the facade last on show?
   a. 1860s
   b. 1900s
   c. 1960s
   d. 1990s

2. Until very recently, why was the King's Cross area not the kind of place you would want to hang around?
   a. It was known for drugs and prostitution.
   b. It was dirty and stinking.
   c. It was dangerous because of the construction work.
   d. It was too crowded.

3. By 2031, how much higher is demand at King's Cross station expected to be?
   a. 10%
   b. 20%
   c. 30%
   d. 40%

What do you remember?

4. What has been bought for King's Cross station with the money invested?

___

5. How many tube lines pass through King's Cross station?

___

6. What wider benefits has the regeneration project brought to the community?

___

●●Background Information●●

　今回紹介されたキングス・クロス駅は、長い歴史を持っています。名前の由来とともに、この駅と周辺地域の歴史を見ていきましょう。

　この駅があるキングス・クロスという地域では、産業化とともに汚染の問題が深刻な問題となりました。その汚名を払しょくしようと、19世紀のジョージ4世統治時代に王（King）の像が十字路（crossroad）に建てられました。しかしあまり出来が良くなかったためか、すぐに取り壊されることとなります。そしてその名前、キングス・クロス（King's Cross）だけがその後残ることとなりました。

　現在のキングス・クロス駅が造られたのは1852年です。これをきっかけに周辺にホテルが建設され、住宅の建設も1850年代後半から始まりました。住居は主に労働者向けのもので、決して質の高いものではなかったようです。この傾向は20世紀になってからも変わらず、ニュースでも触れられていたようにこの地域の治安はあまり良くありませんでした。また、1987年の火災、2005年のキングス・クロス・セント・パンクラス駅近くでのテロにより、危険なエリアというイメージが付いてしまったことも否定できません。

　しかし、2012年のロンドン・オリンピック開催を前に、巨額の費用を費やした再開発が始まります。この再開発は古さと新しさを融合させたイギリスらしいものとなりました。駅舎の再開発はUnit 1で紹介したイングリッシュ・ヘリテッジの協力のもとに行われました。駅の建物は保存指定建造物1級に指定されているものなのです。そして古い建物を維持すると同時に、駅の屋根を利用しようと、ソーラーパネルが設置されることになりました。駅で使われる電力の10パーセントは太陽光発電から得られたものです。駅前に大きな広場もでき、キングス・クロス駅は明るくクリーンなイメージを持つ駅へと変化を遂げました。

参考：http://www.networkrail.co.uk/aspx/6288.aspx
　　　http://www.kingscross.co.uk/19th-century
　　　http://www.visitkingscross.com/history.htm

5 Filling Gaps　　　　　　　　　　　CD1-17 [Original]　CD1-18 [Voiced]

Watch the DVD, then fill the gaps in the text.

Newsreader: Now for years King's Cross station looked like this: green hoarding on the front of a (¹   ) building. And for decades the King's Cross area, for Londoners, was (²   ) with drug dealing and prostitution. But now things have changed, thanks to one of Europe's biggest (³   ) projects. Let's join Alice Bhandhukravi, who can tell us more. Alice.

Alice Bhandhukravi: Liz, this is one of London's busiest stations. Six out of 11 tube lines pass through here, so the (⁴   ) was certainly a long time coming. Now, er, one of the first changes that you will notice: behind me, there, you will see the beautiful facade – it hasn't been on show since the 1860s. The second, er, most (⁵   ) change is this huge square in front of the facade. It used to be a (⁶   ) of entrances. Part of it was within the station so it's all been opened up for people to (⁷   ) easily. The new look station was (⁸   ) opened this morning by the Transport Secretary and Boris Johnson doing the honours.

Bhandhukravi: It opened to fanfare and applause this morning, but of course this station never actually (⁹   ). As regular passengers will know, building work has been taking place all around them for years, creating what the mayor described as a higgledy-piggledy chaos. Today though, he went so far as to call it a (¹⁰   ) of modern design.

Boris Johnson, Mayor of London: The trains, the track, the signalling, that's obviously critical but people need to be able to circulate smoothly, they need to be able to enjoy the space. The ticket hall over there is fantastic and this will help us to (¹¹   ) (¹²   ) a massive increase in ... we're gonna get 30% increase in demand by 2031 in, in King's Cross. Plus, we're gonna have Crossrail too, coming in, (¹³   ) just over there. You're gonna need more space.

Bhandhukravi: But getting more space has

34

taken four years and cost more than half a billion pounds. That's bought a new concourse with shops and cafes, a new glass roof, a (^{14}) facade and, of course, the square in front. As infrastructure programmes go, it's up there with the biggest in Europe.

Female passenger: I haven't been to this area for a long time and I think the whole area is stunning.

Male passenger 1: It feels nice – a place to stay where you can wait for your friends, family, whoever. So yeah it's nice. The whole feel is nice.

Male passenger 2: Really impressive and, um, it, you know it just shows how a gloomy area can be transformed and, um, have some life brought back into it.

Bhandhukravi: So to think that until (^{15}) yesterday, this was a place you wouldn't really want to (^{16}) (^{17}) in. Say ... something famously of a bit of a red-light district, somewhere you wanted to (^{18}) (^{19}) quickly. So the investment, er, has certainly been welcome here. But it's also brought wider (^{20}), uh, to the community as a whole. Private companies have been (^{21}) billions of pounds just to the north of here.

(*Thursday 26 September 2013*)

Notes ....

l. 1: **King's Cross station**「キングス・クロス駅」1852年開業の鉄道ターミナル駅。ロンドン中心部の北に位置する   l. 2: **hoarding**「(建築現場の) 一時的な板囲い」   l. 13: **facade**「(建物の装飾的な) 外面」   l. 17: **Transport Secretary**「運輸大臣」2012年よりパトリック・マクローリン (Patrick McLoughlin 1957-) が務める   l. 18: **Boris Johnson**「ボリス・ジョンソン (1964-)」大ロンドン市長。2008年から現職   l. 22: **a higgledy-piggledy chaos**「混乱でごった返した状態」   l. 30: **Crossrail**「クロスレイル」南東イングランドで建設中の総延長118 kmの鉄道線路   l. 38: **As infrastructure programmes go, it's up there with the biggest in Europe.**「(キングス・クロス駅の改築は) 基本設備 (改築) 計画としては、ヨーロッパ最大のものにあたる。」   l. 47: **a place** これと次の文のsomething, somewhereは全て同格で「キングス・クロス駅周辺地域」を指す   l. 48: **Say**「言わば」挿入的に用いる   l. 49: **famously**「よく知られているように」文修飾の副詞   l. 49: **a red-light district**「売春の多く行われている地域」

Unit 6   *Renovation of King's Cross Station*   **35**

Behind the Scenes

イギリスの鉄道とターミナル駅

　イギリスの鉄道は、1994年より民営化され、名前もかつての「ブリティッシュ・レール」("British Rail")から「ナショナル・レール」("National Rail")*に変わっています。ロンドンには中央駅はなく、主要鉄道幹線の（各）方面別に、中心市街地の外延にターミナル駅がいくつか設けられています。キングス・クロス駅（北部方面）の他には、セント・パンクラス駅（中東部方面、ユーロスターの発着駅）、パディントン駅（西部方面）、ヴィクトリア駅（南東部方面、オリエント急行の発着駅）、ウォータールー駅とチャリング・クロス駅（南部方面）などがあります。『ハリー・ポッター』（キングス・クロス駅の9と3/4番線）や『くまのパディントン』（パディントン駅）など、文学作品にも登場します。

　　*ナショナル・レールは、（それまでの）旧国鉄ブリティッシュ・レールに由来する鉄道網を中心に、旅客列車を現在運行している複数の民間会社の統一ブランドです。

▶▶▶ Moving On

6 Making a Summary

　　　　　　　　　　　　　　　　　　　　　　　　　　　　CD1-19

Fill the gaps to complete the summary.

　　King's Cross station in London was once (a　　　　　) with drug dealing and prostitution. But a major (r　　　　　　) project, costing over half a billion pounds, has (t　　　　　　) the station. There is a new (c　　　　　) with shops and cafes, a new glass roof, a restored facade and a square in front. The project has taken years, and today the Mayor of London described the station as a (m　　　　　) of modern design. (D　　　　　) at King's Cross station is expected to increase by 30% by 2031. This project has brought some additional (b　　　　　) to the community as private companies have been (i　　　　　) billions of pounds just to the north of the station.

7 Follow Up

Discuss, write or present.

1. Is there a run-down building or dilapidated area you would like to see regenerated?
2. Do you know of any major regeneration projects taking place in Japan?
3. Are there any areas in your hometown that are notorious for crime? What could be done to improve them?

Unit 7
Horse Therapy

動物介在療法の一つとして、馬との触れ合いを通じて心的傷害を克服するセラピーがあります。「動物愛護の国」イギリスらしい治療法はどのようにして行われるのでしょうか。

▶ Starting Off

1 Setting the Scene

What do you think?

1. If you are very stressed, what helps you relax?
2. Have you ever had a stressful job? What jobs do you think you would find most stressful?
3. Do you think that being with animals might help people relax? What animals do you think would be most relaxing?

2 Building Language

For each word (1-5), find two synonyms (a-j).

1. hyper-vigilant [/]
2. handle [/]
3. grounded [/]
4. stabilisation [/]
5. ego [/]

a. security
b. balance
c. settled
d. individuality
e. too careful
f. cope with
g. established
h. identity
i. too alert
j. manage

37

▶▶ Watching the News

3 Understanding Check 1

Read the quotes, then watch the DVD and match them to the right people.

1. This work really helps them to sort of feel solid and safe again.　　[　]

2. ... it's helped Hugh Forsyth come to terms with his experiences of serving in Northern Ireland ...　　[　]

3. ... I know for a fact that it works, er, because I've experienced it.　　[　]

4 Understanding Check 2

Which is the best answer?

1. What is 'equine facilitated therapy'?
    a. a remedy for sick horses
    b. a soldier's experience in Northern Ireland
    c. a kind of illness that soldiers often get
    d. a treatment for people with mental and stress problems

2. How did horse therapy cure Hugh Forsyth?
    a. He enjoyed riding the horses very fast.
    b. He learned to be very vigilant with the horses.
    c. He communicated and made a connection with the horses.
    d. He worked in crowds with the horses.

3. What advice does Hugh give to the other man?
    a. Don't worry about making mistakes.
    b. Don't have too much fun.
    c. Learn to be by yourself.
    d. Don't forget that you are a soldier.

What do you remember?

4. What problems did Hugh Forsyth have when he left the army?

   _____

5. How did Hugh start to feel when he began working with horses?

   _____

6. What kind of work does Hugh do with 'Walking with the Wounded'?

   _____

●●Background Information●●

　今回のニュースで扱われたホースセラピーの歴史は古く、古代ギリシャ文学には、乗馬による治療が行われたことが記されています。その後、1946年にスカンジナヴィアでポリオ患者が発生した際、ホースセラピーが導入されました。1960年、アメリカとカナダでCommunity Association for Riding for the Disabled（CARD）という団体がホースセラピーを開始し、1969年、アメリカのミシガン州にCheff Therapeutic Riding Centerが創設されました。同年、コロラド州にNorth American Riding for the Handicapped Association（NARHA）が設立され（2011年にProfessional Association of Therapeutic Horsemanship Internationalと改名）、この団体はホースセラピーの安全ガイドラインや訓練の提供、療法士の資格授与やセンター設立の認可を行っています。

　ニュースに登場したイギリスの団体IFEALは、"Dare to Live"（生きるための挑戦）というトラウマや鬱、不安感を克服するためのプログラムを提供しています。このプログラムは、心理的学習と体験的学習が組み合わされたもので、1日から3日の日程で行われます。乗馬はせず、馬とのふれあいで安心感を促進することが目的です。

　動物を用いたセラピーには、馬以外に、象、イルカ、犬、猫などもありますが、馬が最も人気のある動物です。その理由として、馬は乗り手の行動や感情に敏感に反応する能力をもっているということが挙げられます。現在、ホースセラピーは、戦争体験によるPTSD治療の他、自閉症、認知症、ダウン症の患者に対して、自尊心の回復、ストレス解消、孤独感を癒すなどの様々な効果をもたらすことが期待されています。

参考：http://www.equestriantherapy.com/
　　　http://www.ifeal.me/

5 Filling Gaps

CD1-20 [Original] CD1-21 [Voiced]

Watch the DVD, then fill the gaps in the text.

Newsreader: Well, now for a (¹   ) story of an army veteran from Surrey (²   ) with post-traumatic stress disorder, who says he's (³   ) the illness ... by working ... with horses. It's called equine facilitated therapy and it's helped Hugh Forsyth come to terms with his experiences of serving in Northern Ireland, and also in Bosnia. Sarah Harris has been to meet him.

Sarah Harris: Just walking into an open field was a (⁴   ) experience for Hugh Forsyth when he first left the army, where he worked for years in bomb disposal.

Hugh Forsyth, army veteran: I was very (⁵   ). Um, I was (⁶   ) to go on tubes, um, on the tubes, on, into London. I couldn't (⁷   ) crowds. Um, I was very scared by dustbins, (⁸   ) ...

Forsyth (*whispering to the horse*): Hiya, darling.

Harris: The idea is for Hugh to make a connection and (⁹   ) with the horses. He says when he started this work the (¹⁰   ) within him was almost immediate.

Forsyth: You get a buzz of adrenalin. Er, a really nice warm, calm feeling and you feel really (¹¹   ). I mean literally connected to the ground. And all your stomach muscles and everything (¹²   ), your whole body relaxes and when you have that eye to eye and the body to body (¹³   ) that the horses have with you, um, it's like you're completely zoned. It's just you and them and nothing else matters.

Sun Tui, International Foundation of Equine Assisted Learning (IFEAL): The work ... the (¹⁴   ) that the horses offer, um, to calm these veterans down when especially they've got a lot of, um, (¹⁵   ) war injuries, you know, that they're coming back with. This work really helps them to sort of

40

feel solid and safe again.

Forsyth (*to another man*): It doesn't matter if it goes right or wrong. Just have a go and have ([16]   ) with it. So, off you go. Use your boundary tool and I'll stay with you if you want me to.

Harris: Now through the charity 'Walking With The Wounded', Hugh is making this his ([17]   ), teaching horsemanship skills to other veterans diagnosed with post-traumatic stress disorder like Adam. His ([18]   ) to others is to at least try it.

Forsyth: Give it a go. Have an open mind. Try not let the, the military ([19]   ) get in the way of the possibility that this can heal you, 'cos I know for a fact that it works, er, because I've experienced it.

Forsyth (*to the other man*): You did that. Well done.

Harris: Hugh says every small ([20]   ) is a huge leap forward in the healing process. Sarah Harris, BBC London news.

(*Thursday 17 October 2013*)

Notes

l. 1: **for**「〜について［の話］です」 l. 2: **Surrey**「サリー州」イングランド南西部にある l. 3: **post-traumatic stress disorder**「心的外傷後ストレス障害（PTSD）」 l. 6: **working**「（馬による）療法を行う」このニュースでは、ほとんどの場合、workは「療法」の意味で用いられる l. 6: **equine facilitated therapy**「馬介在療法」動物介在療法の一つ l. 8: **come to terms with**「（困難などを）受け入れる、甘受する」 l. 9: **Bosnia**「ボスニア」バルカン半島西部の地域 l. 11: **when he first left the army**「彼が退役してまもない頃」 l. 20: **adrenalin**「アドレナリン」副腎から分泌されるホルモンで、交感神経の伝達物質としても働く。興奮状態において分泌される l. 25: **zoned**「ぼうっとする［恍惚］状態」 l. 25: **matter**「大事である」 l. 26: **International Foundation of Equine Assisted Learning**「国際馬介在療法財団（IFEAL）」 l. 33: **feel solid**「落ち着いた気持ちになる」 l. 35: **have a go**「やってみる、試してみる」 l. 37: **boundary tool**「（馬に人との）距離の取り方を教えるための道具」堅い棒や縄などを用いることが多い。馬が人間に近づきすぎた場合は、その棒で地面を軽くたたいたり、馬の前に差し出したりして、人間との適切な距離感を友好的な方法で馬に伝える l. 39: **'Walking With The Wounded'**「（戦争で）傷ついた者とともに歩む会」戦争で身体や心に傷を負った退役軍人たちが、軍務以外の仕事に就けるよう支援する慈善活動団体 l. 43: **Try not let** 文法的には、"Try not to let"となるべきところ l. 46: **You did that. Well done.**「できたじゃない。よくやった。」

Behind the Scenes

馬と人間とのより良い関係

　ニュースに登場したヒュー・フォーサイスは、馬との触れ合いにより心の安定を取り戻すことができました。フォーサイスはその後IFEALで、「馬との自然な対話術」(natural horsemanship)、いわゆるhorse whisperingを学んでいます。これは馬を鞭で打つなど体罰でしつけたり、威嚇して恐怖心を与えることで精神的優位に立ったりする方法ではなく、馬の気持ちを理解、尊重し、信頼関係を築き、馬と同じ立場から馬を馴らす方法です。

　馬は精神的な傷を癒してくれる存在です。しかし、馬から癒しを得る大前提として、人間の側も馬の気持ちを理解しようとし、馬が最善の状態でいられるよう最大限の努力とともに接することが必要だということを忘れてはなりません。

▶▶▶ Moving On

6 Making a Summary

CD1-22

Fill the gaps to complete the summary.

　Equine facilitated therapy helps war (v_____) overcome their mental injuries by working with horses. The work (s_____) them and helps them to feel solid and safe. Hugh Forsyth left the army with (p_____) stress disorder, and had become (h_____): he was scared of riding the tube and he couldn't (h_____) crowds. He says that when he started to make a (c_____) with horses, he felt an immediate transformation. He felt warm, relaxed and (g_____), as if nothing else mattered. Now he is teaching horsemanship skills to other (v_____) and his advice is that they should have fun. They should forget their military (e_____) and not worry about making mistakes. He knows it works because he has experienced it.

7 Follow Up

Discuss, write or present.

1. What do you think of equine facilitated therapy? Do you think that it could relax you if you felt very stressed?
2. Can you think of any other useful therapies for stress?
3. Hugh said, "It doesn't matter if it goes right or wrong. Just have a go and have fun with it." Can you think of any other situations where this might be good advice?

Unit 8
Cyber Monday

今年もまた「サイバー・マンデー」がやってきました。商品を売る側にとって、一年で最も重要な日の一つです。一体どんな日なのでしょう。また、どうしてサイバー・マンデーという名前で呼ばれているのでしょう。

▶ Starting Off

1 Setting the Scene

What do you think?

1. How has the way that you do your shopping changed in the last few years?
2. What do you think is the most popular Christmas or New Year gift in Japan? Has this changed in the past few years?
3. When is the busiest shopping day of the year in Japan? Do most people still use shops, or do they do their shopping online?

2 Building Language

Which word or phrase (1-5) best fits which explanation (a-e)?

1. flat out   [ ]   a. an informal word meaning extremely large
2. scale   [ ]   b. the highest, strongest or best point, value or skill
3. whopping   [ ]   c. the size or level of something, particularly when it is large
4. transaction   [ ]   d. at top speed with maximum effort
5. peak   [ ]   e. an occasion when somebody buys or sells something

▶▶ Watching the News

3 Understanding Check 1

Watch the DVD and choose T (true) or F (false) for each question.

1. On Cyber Monday, people do a lot of online shopping, so retailers increase prices.
   [T / F]

2. In summer, there is a big uplift in spending.
   [T / F]

3. In the past three years, the volume of sales from mobile devices has risen a lot.
   [T / F]

4. For many people, Cyber Monday means the beginning of Christmas shopping.
   [T / F]

4 Understanding Check 2

Which is the best answer?

1. Why are the conveyer belts going as fast as possible on Cyber Monday?
   a. Shops are going to reduce their prices and offer big discounts soon.
   b. It is Christmas Day tomorrow.
   c. There are 18 kilometres of conveyer belts.
   d. There were lots of weekend orders, with people spending their pay cheques.

2. Why will there be another spike in online shopping on Christmas Day?
   a. People will be relaxed and in the mood for shopping.
   b. Lots of people will be using their new tablet computers.
   c. Prices will go down.
   d. Retail will be taking a new direction.

3. How many parcels are being sent by the centre every hour?
   a. 1,600
   b. 2,600
   c. 3,600
   d. 4,600

What do you remember?

4. What happened on Black Friday?

5. What has happened to mobile sales recently, and why?

6. When is the busiest time for online shopping on Cyber Monday?

●●Background Information●●

　ブラック・フライデーやサイバー・マンデーは、いずれも伝統的にはアメリカの感謝祭明けに年末セールが開始されることによって、購買力が非常に高まることから名づけられたもので、アメリカに起源があるわけですが、シアトルに本社があるアマゾンやアメリカのウォルマート（Walmart）系列のイギリスのスーパーマーケットであるASDAなどがこの時期のセールを始めたことから、イギリスにも浸透したと考えられます。

　オンライン・ショッピングでは、早朝から夜遅くまで、平日でも休日でも、そして通勤途中、職場や自宅でも、携帯やタブレットを使って自分に都合の良い時間や場所で自由に買い物をすることができます。人混みを避けられることも利点の一つです。サイバー・マンデーにスマートフォンやタブレットを利用しての買い物件数は、2013年は2012年と比べて2倍に増え、オンライン・ショッピング全体でみても、3分の1以上がこうした携帯端末によるものだそうです。買い物の仕方が時代とともに変化しているのが分かります。

　実際のお店を訪れることなく、オンラインでこれだけ便利に買い物ができてしまうと、小売店はどのようにして集客力をあげていけばいいのでしょうか。実は、"click-and-collect"（「（オンラインで）クリックして（注文をし）、（実店舗に商品を）引き取りに行く」）システムが導入され、実店舗からも消費者の足が遠のかないよう、小売店もオンライン・ショッピングとの共存を図ろうとしています。

　クリスマスになるとライトアップされるリージェント・ストリートのイルミネーションの中、大通りに並ぶおもちゃ屋ハムリーズなどのお店がクリスマス・プレゼントを求める人々で賑わう、そうしたクリスマスならではの風景が消えることはないようです。

参考：http://www.telegraph.co.uk/news/uknews/10487092/Online-Christmas-shoppers-prepare-for-record-Cyber-Monday.html
　　　http://www.theguardian.com/business/2013/dec/02/christmas-shopping-cyber-monday-black-friday

5 Filling Gaps

🔘 CD1-23 [Original] 🔘 CD1-24 [Voiced]

Watch the DVD, then fill the gaps in the text.

Newsreader: Now it's thought that around 300,000 pounds is being spent online every minute today, as (¹   ) get down to the business of Christmas shopping. Today has become known as Cyber Monday, the day when retailers slash prices and offer big discounts ahead of Christmas. Some are (²   ) that today could turn out to be the busiest online shopping day in history. Well, our business correspondent, Emma Simpson, is at a big (³   ) centre in Milton Keynes for us now. Emma.

Emma Simpson: Now, just to give you a sense of the (⁴   ) of this place, Sophie, you could fit 14 football pitches in here and there are 18 kilometres of conveyer belts. They're already (⁵   ) (⁶   ), dispatching all the online orders that were made over the weekend, and with pay cheques now in, there's gonna be an awful lot of shopping being done today.

Simpson: The boxes just keep on coming. A mega (⁷   ) humming with activity, where John Lewis is already (⁸   ) (⁹   ).

Mark Lewis, Head of Online, John Lewis: It started really on Friday with what's now known as Black Friday, where we saw twice as much activity on the site as we've seen on any one day before. So what we're seeing is, people are shopping earlier in the morning on their mobile phones. We're also seeing shoppers shop later in the evening, sat at home on the sofa, using a tablet, and shopping as late as 10, 11 o'clock into the evening.

Simpson: Whatever device they're using, it's all about online. Visa Europe (¹⁰   ) 450 million pounds will be spent online today on its cards alone. That's an increase of 18% compared with last year, and a (¹¹   ) 7.7 million (¹²   ), via the net.

Fiona Wilkinson, Director, Visa Europe: All the way through the summer we've seen (¹³   ) being fairly cautious: a little bit of increase in spending, but not very much. It feels now that December is here, just three weeks to go before Christmas, that there really is a big (¹⁴   ).

46

Simpson: Here, it's a high-tech (¹⁵   ) to get the goods out. It's easy to see what's selling. And guess what the most popular item is? The tablet computer. It means that on Christmas Day when they all get opened, there'll be another spike in online shopping.

Simpson: Retail's taking a (¹⁶   ) (¹⁷   ) fast, with tablets and smartphones changing the way we're (¹⁸   ) and (¹⁹   ).

Andrew McClelland, Chief Operations Officer, IMRG: Mobile sales have rocketed over the last three years. We've gone from 1% of total online spent, to 27%. We're all multi-, multitasking now. We're using our devices in different ways. We're watching television. We're using tablets. We're using smartphones.

Simpson: Retailers have had to change their game too, to keep up with this shift. Cyber Monday could turn out to be another record-breaking day for online shopping.

Simpson: Now you can probably see some of those parcels coming down the chutes before they're heading off into lorries. They're (²⁰   ) about one unit, one good, every second here. Now the (²¹   ) for online shopping today is apparently between eight and nine o'clock tonight. So you could say that the starting gun for Christmas shopping has well and truly been fired.

Newsreader: It has, Emma. Thank you very much.

(Monday 2 December 2013)

Notes ···

l. 10: **Milton Keynes**「ミルトン・キーンズ」イングランド中南部の町　l. 17: **humming with activity**「活気づいている」　l. 18: **John Lewis**「ジョン・ルイス」イギリスの百貨店　l. 20: **Black Friday**「ブラック・フライデー」感謝祭（11月の第4木曜日）の翌日の金曜日。クリスマスのセールがこの日から始まる　l. 25: **Visa Europe**「ビザ・ヨーロッパ」クレジットカード会社　l. 31: **three weeks to go**「あと3週間」　l. 38: **spike**「急増、急上昇」　l. 42: **IMRG**「インタラクティブ・メディア・イン・リテール・グループ (Interactive Media in Retail Group)」オンライン・ショッピング業界の団体　l. 44: **multitasking**「複数の作業を同時に処理している」　l. 53: **well and truly**「完全に」

Behind the Scenes

cyberの語源

今回のニュースのキーワードCyber Mondayのcyberの語源について考えてみましょう。cyberという語を最初に使ったのは、アメリカ、マサチューセッツ工科大学のノーバート・ウィーナー（Norbert Wiener, 1894-1964）教授でした。教授は、神経や脳といった生物の制御機構と通信など機械の制御機構の共通原理を究明する学問を、ギリシア語で「船の舵を取る者」を意味する「サイバネティックス」（cybernetics）と名づけました。

その後cyberは「コンピューターの、インターネットの」を意味する接頭辞となり、現在では「サイボーグ」（cyborg）や「サイバースペース」（cyberspace）などの単語に使われています。

▶▶▶ Moving On

6 Making a Summary

CD1-25

Fill the gaps to complete the summary.

There have been huge changes in the (r   ) industry. More people are shopping online, and now more orders are being placed from mobile devices, because people are multitasking: doing many things at the same time. Three weeks before Christmas, on Black Friday, online activity at John Lewis doubled. People placed orders at the weekend, so today, Cyber Monday, there might be a (w   ) 7.7 million (t   ), with 300,000 pounds spent every minute. In a distribution centre of enormous (s   ), the machines are working (f   ) (o   ) until the (p   ) in the evening. Sales also increased because retailers (s   ) prices and offered big discounts. The most popular gift was the tablet computer, so at Christmas there will be another (s   ) in online sales when people use them to place more orders.

7 Follow Up

Discuss, write or present.

1. What are the advantages and disadvantages of shopping online?
2. At the beginning of the unit, you were asked to consider if the way you do your shopping has changed. Were you surprised when you read about how much things have changed in Britain? Do you think Japan is already like that, or will it be like that in the future?
3. Would you like to work in one of those enormous distribution centres? Do you think it would be better or worse than working in a shop?

Unit 9
The Red Cross to Aid Food Poverty

近年、イギリスでは、食事を満足にとれない貧困家庭が増加しているようです。食料難を解決するためにどのような取り組みが行われているのでしょうか。

▶ Starting Off

1 Setting the Scene

What do you think?

1. Many people in the world cannot afford to buy enough food. What countries do you think they are in?
2. What do you think might be good ways to help people who cannot afford to buy their own food?
3. Have you ever tried to help hungry people?

2 Building Language

For each word (1-5), find two synonyms (a-j).

1. struggle   [/   ]
2. donate   [/   ]
3. support   [/   ]
4. humanitarian [/   ]
5. generosity   [/   ]

a. kindness   f. philanthropic
b. battle   g. contribute
c. unselfishness   h. charitable
d. help   i. give
e. have difficulty j. aid

49

▶▶ Watching the News

3 Understanding Check 1

Watch the DVD and choose T (true) or F (false) for each question.

1. The Red Cross is aiming to help people in poverty for the first time ever.

   [T / F]

2. The Red Cross wants to become more involved in food poverty.

   [T / F]

3. The Red Cross is asking people to donate money.

   [T / F]

4. Recently, it has become more difficult for people to buy enough food for their families.

   [T / F]

4 Understanding Check 2

Which is the best answer?

1. How should people donate food?
   a. They should bring food that they don't want and donate it
   b. They should buy more food than they need and then donate it.
   c. They should donate any food that they accidentally bought.
   d. They should skip meals and donate the food they save.

2. According to Dawn Lee from Zap Play Centre, why are people struggling to buy enough food?
   a. They don't have enough money.
   b. They have too many children.
   c. They don't have jobs.
   d. People are not generous enough.

3. In the Tesco poll of 4,000 people, how many people had not been able to buy enough food?
   a. nearly everybody
   b. almost 1,600
   c. more than two-thirds
   d. about 1,300

What do you remember?

4. According to Simon Lewis from the Red Cross, what does the organisation want to be more involved in, and why?

_____

5. Why did the reporter say that Liverpool shoppers were the most generous of all?

_____

6. What was the after-school centre able to do, and why was it important?

_____

●●Background Information●●

　今回のニュースでは、赤十字社が食料不足で困っている人々へのチャリティを呼びかけていました。イギリスでは近年、「フードバンク」と呼ばれるチャリティ団体を利用する人が急増しています。フードバンクは地元のスーパーの入り口で「ショッピングリスト（その時点で必要とされている食料の一覧）」を配布し、その「ショッピングリスト」を見た買い物客がニュースで解説されていたシステムに従って、各自寄付を行います。2012年の4月から9月の6ヶ月間と2013年の同時期でのフードバンクの利用者を比較すると、2013年には3倍となっていることがわかります。イギリスで、いったい何が起きているのでしょうか。

　原因を一つに絞ることはできませんが、挙げられている理由の一つに、2013年4月から福祉政策に転換が見られたこと、特に「寝室税」("Bedroom Tax")の導入があります。これは民間の賃貸住宅ではなく、公営の住宅に住む人々、つまり比較的低所得である人々を対象に導入された税であり、使っていない部屋があると住宅への補助金が減らされるというシステムです。空き部屋一つにつきこれまでの手当てが14％削減され、二部屋以上だと25％削減されます。家賃が払えなければもっと狭い部屋を探して今の部屋を出ていけばいいのかもしれませんが、引っ越すためのお金もない人が多く、問題の解決にはなりません。

　チャリティ先進国と言われるイギリスではありますが、この貧困問題は容易に解決できそうにありません。

参考：http://www.independent.co.uk/news/uk/home-news/hungrier-than-ever-britains-use-of-food-banks-triples-8882340.html
http://www.theguardian.com/society/2013/nov/29/uk-biggest-food-drive-second-world-war-poverty-welfare
http://www.bbc.com/news/uk-politics-26148099

5 Filling Gaps

CD2-02 [Original]   CD2-03 [Voiced]

Watch the DVD, then fill the gaps in the text.

Newsreader: Here, for the first time since the Second World War, the Red Cross is to collect food (¹   ) to go to families (²   ) to feed themselves. It's joined two other charities, asking people to (³   ) food as they go the, go to the supermarket to buy food. Latest figures suggest that nearly half a million people in Britain needed (⁴   ) from food banks last year. Emma Simpson reports.

Emma Simpson: Every donation counts, all part of a massive operation to gather food.

Volunteer (*to another man*): There's a big food donation for FareShare.

Simpson: This supermarket chain is (⁵   ) the collection points, and for the first time the Red Cross has decided to (⁶   ) (⁷   ).

Simon Lewis, Red Cross: We're a (⁸   ) organisation. We do many things in the UK. Food (⁹   ) is one of the issues, which has come to the (¹⁰   ) very recently. We think it's a growing issue and it's something that we want to get more involved in: er, helping people in (¹¹   ), which includes the food poverty issue.

Simpson: The idea is (¹²   ). Shoppers are asked to pop a few extra items into their baskets and then drop them off on the way out. And the most (¹³   ) shoppers of all are here in Liverpool.

Simpson: Christmas offers everywhere but not everyone can (¹⁴   ) them. Some people are struggling with the basics. Tesco polled more than 4,000 people and found that almost a third had (¹⁵   ) meals or relied on others to (¹⁶   ) their families over the last year. Forty per cent said their situation had got worse, and almost as many said they would (¹⁷   ) putting the heating on in order to eat.

Dawn Lee, Zap Play Centre (*to children*): Who wants some soup?

Children: Me!

Simpson: At this after-school centre in Liverpool, they're now able to provide some fresh food. A (^18   ) for some, but for others, it's a (^19   ), much needed meal.

Lee: Across the board, there's a lot less money, erm, going into households. Erm, speaking to our parents, erm, they're fi-, they're struggling to be able to keep the same levels of food on the table.

Teacher (*to children*): I think yours might be done.

Simpson: An unexpected treat. The (^20   ) of others can go a long way. The hope is for a mountain of food to be (^21   ) by the end of this weekend. Emma Simpson, BBC news, Liverpool.

(*Friday 29 November 2013*)

Notes
l. 2: **the Red Cross**「赤十字社」世界中で人道的支援を行うボランティア団体　l. 9: **food banks**「フードバンク」寄付された食料を困窮者に配給する活動を行う団体　l. 12: **FareShare**「フェアシェア」イギリスで食料難解決のため活動する慈善団体。フードバンクの一つ　l. 13: **collection points**「(食料)収集所」　l. 22: **Liverpool**「リバプール」イングランド北西部の都市　l. 24: **Tesco**「テスコ」イギリスに本拠地を置く、1919年創業の大手スーパーマーケット・チェーン　l. 38: **Across the board**「全面的に」　l. 42: **go a long way**「大いに役に立つ」

Unit 9　The Red Cross to Aid Food Poverty　53

Behind the Scenes

イギリスのスーパーマーケット

　イギリスの代表的なスーパーマーケットは、テスコ（Tesco）の他にもいくつかあります。まず、上・中流階級を対象としているのは、高級スーパーとされるウェイトローズ（Waitrose）や、衣料品やインテリア用品、食品部門も充実していて百貨店のようなマークス＆スペンサー（Marks & Spencer）です。次に中流階級向けのスーパー、セインズベリー（Sainsbury's）があり、テスコ同様、大型スーパーチェーンで店舗数も多く、価格も標準的で、広く一般に親しまれています（テスコの方が、若干安い価格設定になっています）。最後に低価格スーパーとしては、モリソンズ（Morrisons、大手スーパーのセーフウェイ〈Safeway〉を買収した企業）、アスダ（ASDA）などがあります。

▶▶▶ Moving On

6 Making a Summary

CD2-04

Fill the gaps to complete the summary.

　　　Many people in Britain are so poor that they are (s　　　　　) to buy enough food. There is so much poverty that last year half a million people needed (s　　　　　) from food banks, and a poll found that about 30% had skipped meals, and some even (r　　　　　) turning on heating to save money for food. The Red Cross is a (h　　　　　) organisation that has become (i　　　　　) in this issue. In supermarkets, they are asking shoppers to buy extra items, which they then (d　　　　　) when they leave. It all depends on people's (g　　　　　), and the shoppers of Liverpool are the most (g　　　　　). The Red Cross then gives the food to places such as an after-school centre, which provides food to children from poor families who cannot (a　　　　　) to buy enough food.

7 Follow Up

Discuss, write or present.

1. At the beginning of this unit, you were asked to think about ways to help people who cannot afford to buy food. What do you think of the Red Cross's solution? Does it seem like an effective one?

2. If you were asked to donate food in this way, how would you feel? Would you do it?

3. Do you think that there is a similar problem in Japan? Are you aware of any special schemes to help poor people who need food in this country?

Unit 10
Bike Hire Scheme

ロンドン市長が公共自転車レンタルシステムの拡大を推進していますが、その前途は多難なようです。市の自転車政策の未来はどうなってしまうのでしょうか。

▶ Starting Off

1 Setting the Scene

What do you think?

1. Are Japanese cities bicycle friendly?
2. How do you travel to work or school, or around the place you live?
3. Does the Mayor or Mayoress of your hometown have any schemes he or she is trying to introduce?

2 Building Language

Which word (1-5) best fits which explanation (a-e)?

1. extend   [　]   a. famous or well known for a negative reason
2. flagship   [　]   b. too full of something
3. congested   [　]   c. make longer or wider
4. contribute [　]   d. give towards something
5. notorious   [　]   e. the main or most important thing

55

▶▶ Watching the News

3 Understanding Check 1

Read the quotes, then watch the DVD and match them to the right people.

1. ... I think we had a great year last year 'cos we had the Olympics and we had the Jubilee. [ ]

2. We have one of the youngest populations, um, anywhere, in, in Europe ... [ ]

3. Why aren't they in Brixton though? I live in Brixton. [ ]

4. ... also funds from elsewhere, to see what we can do to expand the cycle hire scheme in places where people really want it. [ ]

4 Understanding Check 2

Which is the best answer?

1. What did Barclays Bank recently announce?
   a. An investment in the bicycle hire scheme.
   b. They are going to withdraw their sponsorship.
   c. They are going to extend their sponsorship.
   d. Free bicycle hire for Barclays' customers.

2. After the expansion, how many more bikes and docking stations will there be?
   a. 2,000 more bikes and 150 new docking stations
   b. 150 more bikes and 2,000 new docking stations
   c. 2,000 more bikes and 1,000 new docking stations
   d. 1,000 more bikes and 150 new docking stations

3. How many trips have been made this year?
   a. 660,000
   b. 500,000
   c. 7,000,000
   d. 7,500,000

What do you remember?

4. Why is the Mayor not concerned that the number of people using the bicycle hire scheme is going down?

   _____

5. Why does Russell King think Wandsworth is perfect for the bicycle scheme?

   _____

6. What is being trialled at the Bow roundabout?

   _____

●●Background Information●●

　2010年5月に、ロンドン市長ボリス・ジョンソンは「ロンドン自転車革命」(London Cycle Revolution) を提言し、その実現のために、同年7月から「ロンドン自転車専用レーン網」(Barclays Cycle Superhighways) と「バークレイズ・サイクル・ハイヤー」(Barclays Cycle Hire) のサービスを開始しました。これは、ロンドン市街の560ヶ所に設置されたドッキング・ステーションのどこでも借り、返却できるレンタル自転車のシステムです。大勢で自転車を共同利用するサイクルシェアリングを実現する仕組みで、交通渋滞の緩和を図り、環境にもやさしく、市民の健康増進にもつながると考えられています。料金は、自転車を借りるときに、自転車のレンタル利用権（24時間2ポンド、1週間で10ポンド）を支払います。そこに30分以上の利用については利用時間に応じて料金が加わり、返却時にその分を清算します。30分以内の利用は課金されないので、（利用権の有効期間内に）短い区間を何度も利用すれば、お金があまりかからず、とても便利です。

　今回のニュースでは、バークレイズの契約打ち切りについて言及されていました。当初は、2015年8月までに2,500万ポンドの資金を、そして2011年の契約更新時には2018年までに2,500万ポンドの追加資金を援助することになっていたのですが、そのスポンサー契約を2016年以降更新しないことを明らかにしたのです。バークレイズはその理由をはっきりとは述べていませんが、ロンドン市内での自転車事故が多発していること、2013年7月にこのレンタル自転車による自転車事故があったことが影響していると言われています。事業拡充には巨額の費用が必要で、ロンドン交通局は新たなスポンサーを探しています。

　また市では、安全な自転車利用のために、自転車が他の車両（特に大型貨物車両）と接触しないような、交差点内の自転車レーンの道幅改善、縁石で分離された自転車道、（交差点で）自転車だけ先に発進させるための信号（"early-start" traffic signals）など様々な案が検討されています。

参考：http://www.bbc.co.uk/news.uk-england-london-25330644
　　　http://www/mirror/co.uk/news/uk-news/boris-bikes-barclays-end-sponsorship-2913543
　　　http://www.tfl.gov.uk/assets/downloads/cycleusers/gla-mayors-cycle-vision-2013.pdf

5 Filling Gaps

CD2-05 [Original]   CD2-06 [Voiced]

Watch the DVD, then fill the gaps in the text.

Newsreader: Boris Johnson's bike hire scheme has been (¹   ) to South West London. Up to 150 docking stations have been (²   ) in Wandsworth and Hammersmith & Fulham. The (³   ) comes days after Barclays announced it will not be renewing its sponsorship of the scheme after 2015. Our transport correspondent, Tom Edwards, has this report.

Tom Edwards: The Mayor's (⁴   ) bike hire scheme today just (⁵   ) (⁶   ). Two thousand more bikes and 150 new docking stations, as it moved into Wandsworth and Hammersmith.

Man: A lot of people do (⁷   ) round here. Um, so yeah, it could be popular.

Woman: It's brilliant. Should be everywhere. Why aren't they in Brixton though? I live in Brixton.

Edwards: Although there have been over seven and a half million trips this year, (⁸   ) (⁹   ) are down and this expansion comes days after it was (¹⁰   ) the main sponsor would be (¹¹   ) (¹²   ) in 2015.

Edwards: The numbers have been going down, is that a (¹³   )?

Boris Johnson, Mayor of London: Not at all. I mean, I think we had a great year last year 'cos we had the Olympics and we had the Jubilee. Obviously we've had to change the er ... the, the, the (¹⁴   ) package and all the rest of it – the pricing. Er, but you know it was getting 660,000 users a month.

Edwards: Wandsworth and Hammersmith councils both (¹⁵   ) two million pounds from planning cash and (¹⁶   ) (¹⁷   ), respectively, to help pay for the expansion.

Russell King, Conservative, Wandsworth Council: We have one of the youngest populations, um, anywhere, in, in Europe quite frankly. Um, so, from a Wandsworth perspective, our demographic is perfect for it.

Nicholas Botterill, Conservative, Hammersmith & Fulham Council: Hammersmith and Fulham's a very (^{18}) borough and, it's very difficult to get around, whether by bus or car and these bikes are gonna be really, really useful.

Edwards: Now though, if the hire scheme (^{19}) further, TFL is looking at other ways to try and pay for it.

Leon Daniels, Transport for London (TFL): We're not planning any further TFL-funded, er, cycle hire expansion. Er, what we'd like to do now is, for business and for the boroughs, to (^{20}) (^{21}) and tell us where they'd like these schemes to be and let's see if we can get a plan together, perhaps out of sponsorship, also funds from elsewhere, to see what we can do to expand the cycle hire scheme in places where people really want it.

Edwards: Elsewhere the Department for Transport is now allowing (^{22}) of lower lights for cyclists at the (^{23}) Bow roundabout. Eleven sites will follow, all part of efforts to try and make London's streets (^{24}). Tom Edwards, BBC London News.

(Friday 13 December 2013)

Notes

l. 1: **Boris Johnson**「ボリス・ジョンソン（1964- ）」大ロンドン市長　l. 1: **bike hire scheme**「公共自転車レンタルシステム」ロンドン交通局が管理する公共の自転車レンタルシステム　l. 3: **docking stations**「自転車の駐輪場」　l. 4: **Wandsworth**「ワンズワース」ロンドン南部の区　l. 5: **Hammersmith & Fulham**「ハマースミス・アンド・フラム」ロンドン西部にある特別区の1つ　l. 6: **comes** 現在形だが、内容は過去のこと。ニュース英語ではしばしば見られる表現　l. 6: **Barclays**「バークレイズ」イギリスに拠点を置く金融大手。公共自転車レンタルシステムのスポンサー　l. 13: **round** 本来ならば around　l. 15: **Brixton**「ブリクストン」ロンドン南にある地域。地下鉄ヴィクトリアラインの終点の駅　l. 17: **trip**「移動」　l. 31: **demographic**「人口統計」　l. 38: **TFL（Transport for London）**「ロンドン交通局」　l. 47: **the Department for Transport**「交通省」ロンドン交通局と異なり、国が管轄する組織　l. 48: **Bow roundabout**「ボウ環状交差路（ラウンドアバウト）」 **roundabout** は「環状交差路、ラウンドアバウト」の意味で、信号のない円形の交差点。一方向に進行し、左折、右折、直進もすべて同時進行で行われる

Behind the Scenes

自転車の歴史

　自転車の歴史は、1817年にドイツのカール・フォン・ドライスが、ハンドルと同じ直径の2つの車輪のついた木製の乗り物を発明したのが始まりです。その後、フランスで改良が加えられ、1870年頃イギリスのジェームズ・スターレーが「ペニー・ファージング型」(Penny Farthing) と呼ばれる前後の車輪の大きさが異なる自転車を発表しました。1879年には、イギリスのヘンリー・ジョン・ローソンが「2つの小輪」を意味する「ビシクレット型」(Bicyclette) の自転車を発明し、これが後に英語のbicycleになりました。

　イギリス人にとって自転車は得意なスポーツの一つであり、近年のオリンピック自転車競技やツール・ド・フランスの優勝者は、イギリス人によって占められています。

▶▶▶ Moving On

6 Making a Summary

CD2-07

Fill the gaps to complete the summary.

　The Mayor of London's (f　　　　) bicycle hire scheme is to be (e　　　　) to the boroughs of Wandsworth and Hammersmith. There will be 2,000 more bicycles and 150 new (d　　　　) stations. This news comes despite the (a　　　　) that Barclays Bank will not renew its sponsorship after 2015. Wandsworth and Hammersmith borough councils have both (c　　　　) to the scheme, in the hope it will be popular with residents and help to ease traffic (c　　　　). The Department of Transport is trying to make London's roads safer for cyclists by (t　　　　) lower lights at the (n　　　　) Bow roundabout.

7 Follow Up

Discuss, write or present.

1. Would you like to have a bicycle hire scheme in your hometown? Do you think it would be popular?
2. Can you think of any other ways traffic congestion problems can be solved?
3. Are the roads in your hometown safe? What could be done to make them safer?

Unit 11
Processed Meat Linked to Early Death

ベーコンやソーセージの食べ過ぎは、早死にすることにつながるかもしれません。加工肉が体に及ぼす悪影響、そして毎日どれぐらいまでは食べていいのか、学んでみましょう。

▶ Starting Off

1 Setting the Scene

What do you think?

1. How much processed meat do you eat each week?
2. Do you eat a healthy diet? How could it be improved?
3. Have you ever travelled to other countries? How do you think their diet compares to the average Japanese person's diet?

2 Building Language

Which word (1-5) best fits which explanation (a-e)?

1. impact   [ ]   a. stop something from happening
2. prevent   [ ]   b. something that influences a result
3. adjust   [ ]   c. facts or information that supports a claim
4. factor   [ ]   d. alter or change slightly
5. evidence [ ]   e. the effect or influence of one thing on another

▶▶ Watching the News

3 Understanding Check 1

Read the quotes, then watch the DVD and match them to the right people.

1. I believe that oily fish is good for you and that bacon is bad. [ ]

2. The issue was putting two bodies of knowledge … together. [ ]

3. Saturated fat is linked to raise LDL cholesterol levels, the bad cholesterol. [ ]

4. … I think every, everybody could cut down, couldn't they? [ ]

4 Understanding Check 2

Which is the best answer?

1. According to the report, what is hypertension caused by?
    a. eating too much meat
    b. eating too much salt
    c. eating too much saturated fat
    d. not eating enough plants

2. How many people, from how many different European countries were followed in this study?
    a. one million people from 13 European countries
    b. half a million people from 13 European countries
    c. half a million people from 10 European countries
    d. half a million people from 30 European countries

3. What is the government's recommendation about the amount of processed meat a person should eat?
    a. at least 160 grams a day
    b. less than 160 grams a day
    c. at least 70 grams a day
    d. less than 70 grams a day

What do you remember?

4. What are some examples of processed meat mentioned in the clip?

5. What was the recommendation of Professor Tim Laing?

6. What other factors are strongly associated with eating lots of processed meat?

●●Background Information●●

　今回のニュースは、加工肉を多量に食べると早死にする可能性が高まるというものでしたが、より具体的には、加工肉と膵臓がん (pancreatic cancer) の関係性についての研究が発表されています。スウェーデンのカロリンスカ研究所のスザンナ・ラーソン教授は、11の実験により、膵臓がんの6643人の患者からデータを取りました。この研究によると、加工肉を1日に50グラム多く食べると、膵臓がんの危険性は19％増え、加工肉を100グラム多く食べると、危険性は38％増えるそうです。

　しかし、「世界がん研究基金」(World Cancer Research Fund) と「国民保健サービス」(NHS: National Health Service) は、この結果に懐疑的です。その理由は、そもそも膵臓がんを発症する患者は少なく（男性77人に1人、女性79人に1人）、また、膵臓がんの発症には、加工肉よりも肥満の方が大きく関係している、というものです。

　一方、肉食と腸がん (bowel cancer) の関係性はすでに認められており、「世界がん研究基金」は、加工肉の代わりに、野菜、豆、卵、チーズ、魚、鶏肉を食べることを推奨しています。いずれにせよ、加工肉の摂取を控えることが健康につながるのは、間違いなさそうです。

参考：http://www.bbc.com/news/health-16526695
　　　http://www.nhs.uk/news/2012/01January/Pages/pancreas-cancer-risk-processed-meat.aspx
　　　http://www.wcrf-uk.org/cancer_prevention/recommendations/meat_and_cancer.php

5 Filling Gaps

CD2-08 [Original] CD2-09 [Voiced]

Watch the DVD, then fill the gaps in the text.

Newsreader: A major study of half a million people across Europe has found further (¹   ) that eating processed meat, such as bacon and (²   ), increases the risk of an (³   ) (⁴   ). As our health correspondent, Dominic Hughes, reports, researchers say reducing the amount we eat could save thousands of lives every year.

Dominic Hughes: People who eat a lot of processed meat that has been preserved, cured or (⁵   ), like bacon, salami, ham or sausage, often have less healthy lifestyles. They (⁶   ) more and tend to be overweight. But even taking these factors into account, a new study seems to show the more processed meat someone eats, the greater their chance of early death.

Victoria Taylor, Dietician, British Heart Foundation: It's likely that the issue with processed meat is to do with the saturated fat and salt content of it. Saturated fat is linked to raised LDL cholesterol levels, the bad cholesterol. And too much salt is linked to hypertension, raised blood pressure.

Hughes: This study followed nearly half a million people, from 10 different European countries, for roughly 13 years. It (⁷   ) in particular on the (⁸   ) processed meat had on their (⁹   ).

Hughes: Those who ate more than 160 grams of processed meat every day, (¹⁰   ) one sausage and three pieces of bacon, were 44% more likely to die. The government (¹¹   ) eating no more than 70 grams a day, around two slices of bacon. And this report says if we eat just 20 grams of processed meat – one small slice of bacon – then 3% of deaths could be (¹²   ). And this is not the first study to (¹³   ) (¹⁴   ) these risks.

Professor Tim Laing, Centre for Food Policy, City University: The issue was putting two bodies of knowledge – cancer and heart disease – together. And still the same (¹⁵   ) came out:

processed meat products. Eat less, eat more plants. That's the issue.

Hughes: But today in Manchester many shoppers took the view this was a case of all things in moderation.

Female shopper 1: I think if you eat it in proportion then, you know, it's not really a big, a big thing really.

Hughes: So I see you've got, um, a kipper, that's a kipper in your bag.

Male shopper: I believe that oily fish is good for you and that bacon is bad, although not as bad as all that – not like cigarettes.

Female shopper 2: With (^{16}) kids in the house, yes, obviously we don't have cooked breakfasts every morning or anything like that. But yeah, yeah I think every, everybody could cut down, couldn't they?

Hughes: Some experts say factors such as smoking, strongly (^{17}) with eating lots of processed meat, have such a powerful impact on (^{18}) health, it's hard to (^{19}) for them. And while many may find this study's recommendations (^{20}) to swallow, the evidence is mounting that too much processed meat is probably not good for your health. Dominic Hughes, BBC News.

(Thursday 7 March 2013)

Notes

l. 3: **processed meat**「加工肉」 l. 15: **British Heart Foundation**「英国心臓財団」 l. 16: **saturated fat**「飽和脂肪」 l. 17: **LDL (＝low-density lipoprotein) cholesterol**「LDLコレステロール」LDL（低密度リポタンパク）に包まれたコレステロールを意味し、悪玉コレステロールのこと l. 18: **hypertension**「高血圧」 l. 24: **no more than**「わずか、たった」 l. 29: **Centre for Food Policy, City University**「ロンドン市立大学の食料政策センター」 l. 35: **plants**「（広い意味で）野菜」 l. 35: **issue**「（問題の）核心」 l. 36: **Manchester**「マンチェスター」イングランド北西部の都市 l. 38: **all things in moderation**「何事もほどほどに」諺としては"Moderation in all things."の形で用いられる l. 39: **in proportion**「分別をわきまえて」 l. 41: **kipper**「ニシン（herring）などの薫製、キッパー」英国ではよく朝食に食べる l. 43: **not as bad as all that**「そんなに悪くはない」

Behind the Scenes

イギリスにおける「肉」騒動

　2013年はイギリスの食肉業界に衝撃が走った年でした。加工肉の危険性が指摘されただけでなく、悪質な偽装が横行していることが発覚したのです。スーパーで売られているハンバーガーやラザニアの牛肉に、イギリス人が食べる習慣のない馬肉が混ざっていることが判明し、しかもその肉には有害な化学物質が含まれていることがわかりました。偽装問題はその後ヨーロッパでも波紋を呼びます。イスラム教徒向けの食品に、宗教上の理由によりイスラム教徒は決して口にすることのない豚肉が混ざっていたことが判明したのです。
　狂牛病問題以降、消費者はますます食肉の安全性に対して過敏になっています。2011年にはイギリスの料理人ジェイミー・オリヴァーが自身の番組で、ハンバーガーに使われる肉に化学薬品が大量に使われていることを指摘しました。今回の加工肉のニュース、そして偽装問題をきっかけに、イギリス人の食肉に対する意識はますます高くなりそうです。

▶▶▶ Moving On

6 Making a Summary

CD2-10

Fill the gaps to complete the summary.

　　A major study of half a million people across Europe has found (e　　　　) that eating (p　　　　) meat increases the risk of an early death. One expert says that it is the amount of (s　　　　) fat and salt found in processed meat that causes health problems. The study (f　　　　) that people who ate more than 160 grams of processed meat every day were 44% more likely to die. The government (r　　　　　　) eating no more than 70 grams a day. Experts say that eating lots of processed meat is associated with other (f　　　　), which have a severe (i　　　　) on a person's health, such as smoking, and it is hard to (a　　　　) for them. One expert suggests that eating more plants and less processed meat may help to (p　　　　) a number of health problems.

7 Follow Up

Discuss, write or present.

1. Is the average Japanese diet improving or getting worse?
2. A good diet is important for a person's overall health. What other factors are important?
3. Women tend to live longer than men. Is this because women tend to eat better? Are there any other factors?

Unit 12
Nursery Ratios Changed to Cut Fees

保護者が負担する保育費を減らすために、政府は新たな方策を提案しました。今後、イギリスの幼児保育はどう変化するのでしょうか。

▶ Starting Off

1 Setting the Scene

What do you think?

1. Can you remember going to nursery school? If so, was it a good experience?
2. Do many parents in Japan send their young children to nursery school? Do you think that this is good or bad for the children?
3. What do parents have to consider when they send their children to nursery school? For example, do they worry about the cost or the staff's qualifications?

2 Building Language

For each word (1-6), find two synonyms (a-l).

1. shake-up   [/]
2. hard-pressed [/]
3. untenable   [/]
4. entertain   [/]
5. standards   [/]
6. proposal   [/]

a. quality
b. anxious
c. unsupportable
d. stressed
e. recommendation
f. values
g. suggestion
h. contemplate
i. illogical
j. consider
k. upheaval
l. transformation

▶▶ Watching the News

3 Understanding Check 1

Read the quotes, then watch the DVD and match them to the right people.

1. I would love to go back to work ... [   ]

2. It will take time to recruit new people. [   ]

3. ... many women are put off going back to work because of the costs. [   ]

4. I'm not particularly in favour of it. [   ]

4 Understanding Check 2

Which is the best answer?

1. What changes has the government proposed?
   a. Staff should be better qualified and have to look after fewer children.
   b. Nursery schools must reduce their prices.
   c. Staff should be allowed to look after more children, but must be better qualified.
   d. Nursery schools must reduce costs by reducing the quality of care.

2. After the changes, how many two-year-olds may an adult look after?
   a. one
   b. two
   c. four
   d. six

3. Why is it difficult for both parents to go to work?
   a. Nursery school staff are not qualified.
   b. Nursery schools are very expensive.
   c. There are too many children in nursery schools.
   d. They are worried about lower standards.

What do you remember?

4. If nursery schools agree to follow the government's proposals, what will they have to do?

___

5. Why do the first parent and Emma Trappet (the last parent) think that they might benefit from the change?

___

6. What is the main concern of the second parent (the father) and Anand Shukler (from the Daycare Trust)?

___

●●Background Information●●

　一人の保育所職員に割り当てる子どもの数を増やすことで保育費の値段を引き下げる今回の試みですが、このニュースから約4ヶ月半後の2013年6月に失敗に終わったことが発表されました。この試みには賛否両論ありましたが、最終的には反対派が勝利したことになります。

　反対の声は、子どもを預ける親、保育所職員たち、専門家からあがりました。職員に割り当てられる子どもが増えることによる保育の質の低下を懸念され、この試みによって保育費が下がるという保証もないという指摘もありました。

　しかし一方で、保育の先進国ともいえるフランスでは、イギリスよりも一人の保育所職員に割り当てられる子どもの数は多く、職員一人に対して1歳以下の子どもは5人、1歳は8人、2歳は8人から12人の割り当てとなっています。数が増えることで質が低下するとは言い切れない面もあるのです。また、収入の低い家庭、シングルペアレントの家庭は保育費が高すぎるために保育所に入れることができず、そのため仕事にもつけないという問題があるのも事実です。2003年以降からの10年間で、家庭の年間の収入は増加していないにもかかわらず、保育費は77％も値上がりしました。家計の27％を保育費に費やしている家庭もあるようです。これはフランスの平均が11％であるのに比べ、大きな違いと言えるでしょう。特に保育費が高いのはロンドン、イングランド東部、イングランド南西部です。

　今回の変更は、ヨーロッパで高い保育の水準を保っているフランスやスウェーデンに追いつくためのものだったのですが、もう一度見直しを迫られました。

参考：http://www.bbc.co.uk/news/education-22782690
　　　http://www.bbc.co.uk/news/education-22854911
　　　http://fct.ritdns.com/childcare-costs-surveys
　　　https://www.gov.uk/government/uploads/system/uploads/attachment_data/file/219660/More_20Great_20Childcare_20v2.pdf

5 **Filling Gaps** CD2-11 [Original] CD2-12 [Voiced]

Watch the DVD, then fill the gaps in the text.

Newsreader: The government is proposing a (¹   ) of nursery provision in England to increase the number of babies and children that can be looked after by a single adult. It's promising better (²   ) staff and lower costs as a result. But there are concerns that the quality of care will (³   ) and that any savings may not be (⁴   ) (⁵   ) to parents. Our education correspondent, Reeta Chakrabarti, has the details.

Reeta Chakrabarti: (⁶   ) a better childcare system for parents is anything but child's play. Costs in the UK are amongst the highest anywhere. Today, the government presented plans it says will help (⁷   ) families.

Chakrabarti: From September nurseries in England will have the (⁸   ) of looking after more children than now, but only if the (⁹   ) is more highly qualified. Salaries will go up but fewer staff could mean a saving for families.

Elizabeth Truss MP, Children's Minister: It will make it higher quality, more (¹⁰   ) and more (¹¹   ). This will take time. It will take time to recruit new people. It will take time to expand nurseries.

Chakrabarti: So what do parents at this South London nursery make of relaxing the ratios?

Parent 1: I would think there will be a welcome change. I think that the nursery costs are really (¹²   ) high. Er, I mean, basically you can't afford to have two parents going to work. The costs of having a full-time nursery are simply too high.

Parent 2: I'm not particularly in favour of it. Even if they're more (¹³   ) on paper, I just think the more people you have to look after, the less, you know, the less, er, (¹⁴   ) you can give.

Chakrabarti: In England the present ratio in nurseries for one-year-olds and under is one adult to three children. What's (^{15}) is one adult to four children. Two-year-olds at present have one adult to four children and the proposed change is one to six. Last year 25 hours of childcare a week for two-year-olds cost an average of more than 5,000 pounds.

Chakrabarti: Finding good quality childcare is hugely important for parents, but it's expensive and many women are put off going back to work because of the costs. But some fear that government (^{16}) for fewer staff could mean lower (^{17}).

Anand Shukler, Daycare Trust: We would worry that if you had something like six two-year-olds for each worker, rather than four, that we have at the moment, there becomes a practical (^{18}) of how many children anybody can look after, care for, help develop at any one time.

Chakrabarti: Watching closely are mothers like Emma Trappett, who (^{19}) can't afford childcare for her twins.

Emma Trappett: I would love to go back to work but, whilst it is so expensive and sort of uncertain to, you know, have childcare, then it's just something that we can't (^{20}).

Chakrabarti: Better childcare, but at (^{21}) cost to parents: that's the circle that ministers today are trying to square. Reeta Chakrabarti, BBC News.

(Tuesday 29 January 2013)

Notes

l. 2: **nursery provision**「保育規定」 l. 12: **child's play**「ささいなこと」 l. 12: **amongst the highest** = one of the highest l. 43: **many women are put off going back to work**「多くの女性は職場に復帰する気がしなくなっている」 l. 55: **that's the circle that ministers today are trying to square.**「それが、今日の大臣たちが解決しようとしている難問だ。」

Behind the Scenes

イギリスの童謡「マザー・グース」

イギリスの童謡は「ナーサリー・ライム」(nursery rhymes) または「マザー・グース」(Mother Goose) と呼ばれ、なぞなぞ唄、子守唄、遊び唄、早口唄、積み上げ唄など種類も豊富です。イギリスの子どもたちは、家庭、保育所や幼稚園で小さい頃から慣れ親しんでいますが、実は残酷な内容も少なくありません。関所遊び唄（アーチを作って唄の最後で誰かを捕まえる）の一つである「ロンドン橋」("London Bridge Is Falling Down") は、木製だった頃に川の氾濫や火災で橋が崩壊し、石の橋が架けられることになったのですが、そのときに生け贄または不寝の番として人柱を埋めたことが歌詞に入れられたという説があります。"London bridge is falling down, / ... / My fair lady." の "lady" はそのときに犠牲となった女性のことだそうです。

Moving On

6 Making a Summary

CD2-13

Fill the gaps to complete the summary.

The childcare system in England is expensive, and many (h   ) families believe that the prices are (u   ). Some parents find the costs of childcare so high that they cannot even (e   ) the idea of both parents returning to work after having children. The government has (p   ) to solve this problem with a (s   ) of nursery provision. The idea is to reduce costs by allowing staff to look after more children, but only if they become more highly (q   ). However, some people worry that (s   ) might fall, because it is just not practical for staff to look after more children. Also, any reduced costs might not be (p   ) on to parents.

7 Follow Up

Discuss, write or present.

1. Why do you think that the British government considers childcare to be so important? Do you think the same reasons exist in Japan?
2. What qualities do you think are necessary to be able to look after young children properly? Do you think people can be taught these qualities, or do you think they come naturally?
3. How do you think the Japanese childcare system can be improved?

Unit 13
Hope for the Blind

失われた視力の再生を可能にする技術の研究が進められています。現在、研究はどの段階まで進められているのでしょうか。また、どんな人に応用が可能なのでしょう。

▶ Starting Off

1 Setting the Scene

What do you think?

1. If you were a medical researcher, for which diseases would you most want to find a cure?
2. Do you know of anybody who is blind? What do you think their lives must be like?
3. Do you think it will ever be possible to cure blindness?

2 Building Language

Which word (1-5) best fits which explanation (a-e)?

1. breakthrough   [ ]   a. moving an organ or tissue within, or into, somebody's body
2. transplantation [ ]   b. a test to discover how effective or suitable something is
3. degenerative   [ ]   c. causing something to gradually become damaged
4. feasible   [ ]   d. a sudden advance that removes a barrier to progress
5. trial   [ ]   e. possible to be done or made

73

▶▶ Watching the News

3 Understanding Check 1

Read the quotes, then watch the DVD and match them to the right people.

1. ... it shouldn't take us too long to be able to do it with human cells. [ ]

2. Now it's those that are being created here in the lab and transplanted into mice. [ ]

3. ... I'm just going to continue just living my life. [ ]

4. We just looked down the microscope after hours and hours ... [ ]

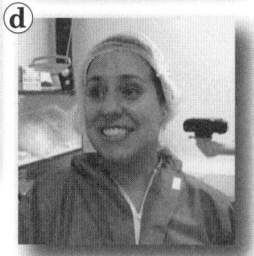

4 Understanding Check 2

Which is the best answer?

1. Why are the scientists calling this event a 'breakthrough'?
   a. They have found the first cure for blindness in humans.
   b. It is the first time blindness has been reversed in mice.
   c. It is the first trial of a new treatment on humans.
   d. They have repaired the sight of mice by using stem cells.

2. When will it be possible to cure humans with this treatment?
   a. within five years
   b. not for many years
   c. soon
   d. when the mice are cured

3. Which blind people might scientists be able to cure?
   a. people who were born blind
   b. all blind people
   c. people who are blind because of degenerative disease
   d. people who have been blind for less than five years

What do you remember?

4. What is the main reason for people losing their sight?

_____

5. Why are the scientists excited?

_____

6. Why isn't Reshi Ramlakhan very excited about the breakthrough?

_____

●●Background Information●●

　今回のニュースは、イギリスのロンドン大学ユニバーシティ・カレッジ（University College London, UCL）のロビン・アリ（Robin Ali）氏の研究チームが、マウスの「光受容細胞に分化させたES細胞」を用いて、失明したマウスの視力を回復させる実験に成功したという内容でした。これまでにES細胞から作製した網膜色素上皮（RPE, retinal pigmented epithelium）によって、失明しかかった患者（ヒト）の視力を回復させたことはありましたが、網膜中の光を捉える光受容細胞に分化させたES細胞での成功は（まだマウスによる実験段階ではありますが）初めてのことです。

　ES細胞を培養して光受容細胞を再形成できたことは、失明を治療するための網膜移植に必要な健康な光受容細胞を数多く供給できる可能性をひらき、大きな期待が寄せられています。この研究が進むことで、失明につながる加齢黄斑変性症（AMD, age-related macular degeneration、加齢に伴い眼の網膜にある黄斑部が変性を起こす病気）やスターガート病（網膜の細胞が傷つきやすくなり、視力が低下する遺伝性の病気）などに苦しむ人々も助けることができると言われています。

　近年、医療の進歩はめざましく、ES細胞やiPS細胞など、再生医療への貢献が期待される様々な発見が続いています。今回の実験では、ES細胞を使った、マウスにおける光受容体の作製に成功しましたが、今後の展望は、受精卵を破壊して作る必要がなく、拒絶反応の可能性も低いとされるiPS細胞を使用して、ヒトに対しても同じ結果が得られるようにすること（臨床応用）です。

　眼を対象とした幹細胞研究が最も進んでいますが、眼が適していることの理由としては、①免疫システムが弱いので、拒絶反応が起きにくい②少しの細胞が回復することで、視力に大きな変化が期待できることが挙げられます。

参考：http://www.independent.co.uk/news/science/cells-to-restore-eyesight-are-grown-in-lab-and-transplanted-into-blind-mice-8725053.html

http://www.afpbb.com/article/life-culture/health/2957177/11067815

5 Filling Gaps

CD2-14 [Original] CD2-15 [Voiced]

Watch the DVD, then fill the gaps in the text.

Newsreader: Scientists in London say they've (¹   ) a (²   ) in research that could help restore the sight of many blind people. A team at University College London and Moorfields have used stem cells to repair the sight of mice. The treatment would only help with certain types of sight loss and could be trialled on humans within five years. Tarah Welsh has more.

Tarah Welsh: They're the blind mice that will be given sight. Scientists have used stem cells to (³   ) the (⁴   ) light-sensing cells in the eye, repairing its retina so it can see. It's being described as a (⁵   ) (⁶   ) in science.

Dr Anai Gonzalez, UCL and Moorfields: We just looked down the microscope after hours and hours, er, working on these cells and it was really exciting.

Welsh: If the stem cell treatment were to work in humans, it could reverse sight loss for the majority of those affected by blindness.

Welsh: More than half of people registered blind have lost their sight through disease, and that's because the photoreceptors which are in the retina at the back of the eye have (⁷   ). Now it's those that are being created here in the lab and transplanted into mice. Blindness has been reversed in mice before using a donor system, which wouldn't be (⁸   ) in people. So this is the first time (⁹   ) (¹⁰   ) are a realistic (¹¹   ).

Professor Robin Ali, UCL and Moorfields: I think what's really exciting about this study is that we now have a route-map, um, for (¹²   ) of embryonic stem cell derived photoreceptors for repairing the retina. And now we've done, shown that we can do it with, with mouse embryonic stem cells, um, it shouldn't take us too long to be able to do it with human cells.

Welsh: Even if this does work in humans, not every blind person would (¹³   ): only those with (¹⁴   ) (¹⁵   ). Reshi is one of them. He has *retinitis pigmentosa*, which means his sight is

76

getting worse and he's likely to lose it completely.

Reshi Ramlakhan: I probably won't get overly excited until, metaphorically speaking, I opened up a newspaper, and in the headlines it said, there's a (^{16}) for RP. Until then, I'm just going to continue just living my life.

Welsh: And (^{17}) (^{18}) from the RNIB.

Clara Eaglen, Royal National Institute of Blind People (RNIB): Well, it's great news. It will be years until this could actually be used in patients so we want to be cautious. However, it could mean that now patients can have sight restored where's there currently no treatment, and just a little bit of extra sight can (^{19}) all the (^{20}). It means they can get out and about and not be isolated.

Welsh: Doctors accept a clinical trial won't (^{21}) (^{22}) for several years but say they're excited that the prospect of reversing blindness is now a reality. Tarah Welsh, BBC London News.

(Monday 22 July 2013)

Notes

l. 4: **A team at University College London and Moorfields**「ロンドン大学ユニバーシティ・カレッジとムーアフィールズ（眼科病院）のチーム」 l. 6: **stem cells**「幹細胞」分裂により同じ細胞を作る能力、また様々な細胞に分化する能力を持っている。これを用いると、こわれた組織や臓器の再生が可能になる l. 12: **retina**「網膜」 l. 16: **reverse sight loss**「失われた視力を回復させる」 l. 17: **affected**「（病気などに）冒される」 l. 19: **photoreceptors**「光受容細胞」生物の組織の一つで、光を感知する l. 22: **donor system**「ドナーシステム」このシステムで視力を再生する場合は、他の人間の神経細胞（視覚に関わる）を用いる。今回の実験で移植された細胞は、他の人間の受精卵を用いたものだが、いろいろな臓器の細胞に分化させられる可能性を持つ分、幅広く患者に適合し、治療に役立てられる可能性がある l. 26: **we now have a route-map**「今、私たちには（この研究がどう進むかの）ルートマップ［経路図］がある」 l. 27: **embryonic stem cell**「胚性幹細胞（ES細胞）」幹細胞の一種。受精卵から胚盤胞に至るまでに発生した胚から得られ、様々な臓器の細胞を作ることができる万能細胞 l. 27: **derived**「由来の」 l. 32: ***retinitis pigmentosa***「網膜色素変性症」目の中にある網膜に異常が生じる遺伝性、進行性の病気。病気の進行とともに、徐々に視力が低下する l. 36: **metaphorically speaking**「例えて言うならば」 l. 40: **RNIB**「英国王立視覚障害者協会（Royal National Institute of Blind People）」 l. 47: **clinical trial**「治験」治療を兼ねた試験。新薬の開発の目的のために行われる

Behind the Scenes

イギリスの再生医療研究―クローン羊のドリー

　イギリスは再生医療の先進国とされますが、これまでに行われた有名な研究に「クローン羊のドリー(Dolly)」があります。ドリーは、スコットランドのロスリン研究所で1996年にクローン技術を用いて誕生しました。ドリーは世界初の哺乳類の体細胞クローンとして、6歳の雌羊の乳腺細胞を、核を除去した未受精卵に移植して生み出されました。しかし、6歳の羊から作られたドリーは、誕生時にすでに遺伝子が6歳であり、生まれつき老化していたとも考えられます。5歳の時に、異常な若さで関節炎を発症し、その後、進行性の肺疾患を起こしたため、2003年に安楽死させられました。死後、ドリーの剥製はエディンバラのスコットランド博物館に展示されています。

▶▶▶ Moving On

6 Making a Summary

CD2-16

Fill the gaps to complete the summary.

　Most blind people are blind because disease has caused the photoreceptors in the (r_____) at the back of their eyes to (d_____). Scientists who are (r_____) on mice have made a (b_____). They have managed to repair the sight of blind mice by (t_____) photoreceptors that are (d_____) from stem cells. This is not the first time they have cured blindness in mice, but this is the first time that the cure has become (f_____) for humans. They could begin (t_____) on humans within five years. However, they will only be able to cure those people who are blind due to (d_____) disease. As it will still be years before there is a cure, one person who is going blind is not getting excited yet.

7 Follow Up

Discuss, write or present.

1. How do you think you would feel if you were going blind, and heard that there might be a cure in a few years?
2. A lot of people say that we should not use animals in medical experiments as it is cruel. What do you think?
3. This story is all about scientists hoping to cure blindness by using stem cells. However, there is hope that stem cell therapy will be able to help cure many other diseases and disabilities. Search the internet to find out about this.

Unit 14
Being British

イギリスでは、どれぐらいの人が自分を「イギリス人」であると思っているのでしょうか。4つの国から成るイギリスにおける国民意識について、学んでみましょう。

▶ Starting Off

1 Setting the Scene

What do you think?

1. Do you feel Japanese or Asian, or both?
2. Do you think that some people who come from, for example, Hokkaido, would feel that being from Hokkaido is more important than being Japanese?
3. Some people who were born abroad have immigrated to Japan and have become Japanese citizens, with Japanese passports. Do you think they feel Japanese? Do you consider them to be Japanese?

2 Building Language

Which word (1-5) best fits which explanation (a-e)?

1. identity   [ ]   a. a range of many things or people different from each other
2. patriotism   [ ]   b. the distinguishing character or personality of an individual
3. ethnicity   [ ]   c. containing people of many different types and cultures
4. diversity   [ ]   d. the love that people feel for their country
5. cosmopolitan   [ ]   e. membership of a particular cultural or national group

▶▶ Watching the News

3 Understanding Check 1

Read the quotes, then watch the DVD and match them to the right people.

1. People who live in Wales and Scotland call themselves Welsh and Scottish . . . [ ]

2. . . . working-age adults are much more likely to say they're British than pensioners. [ ]

3. I still class myself as British, Indian. [ ]

4. Britain is, um, three or four different countries now. [ ]

4 Understanding Check 2

Which is the best answer?

1. What percentage of white Britons describe themselves as British?
   a. 40%
   b. 14%
   c. 13%
   d. 30%

2. Why is Harrow considered to be the most British place in Britain?
   a. Winston Churchill studied there.
   b. The people come from many different cultural backgrounds.
   c. Most of the people are black.
   d. There are lots of English people living there.

3. The people of which section of the population are most likely to describe themselves as British?
   a. white British
   b. black people
   c. Asian people
   d. over-75s

What do you remember?

4. Where was the Indian wedding, and what music was being played there?

　

5. Which generation are least likely to describe themselves as British?

　

6. What did the second man interviewed in the pub think about ethnic minorities?

　

●●Background Information●●

　今回のニュースの題材となったのは、2011年3月27日にイギリスで行われた国勢調査のアンケート結果でした。国勢調査は古来、税金や兵力の算出のために各国で行われており、イギリスでは、1801年に開始されました。1911年の調査は、仕事や業種、地位など1ページに収まるほどの質問を通じて、国民の貧困率や栄養状態、幼児の致死率を把握しようとしました。一方、2011年度版は、仕事や就業について15問、家庭について14問、個人的な質問40問など、その質問数が大幅に増加し、30ページにものぼるものでした。

　2011年に初めて設けられたナショナル・アイデンティティについての質問では、イングランドとウェールズで調査を受けた5600万人の91％が、何らかの「イギリス」のアイデンティティ（イングランド人、ウェールズ人、スコットランド人、北アイルランド人、もしくはイギリス人）を選びました。イングランドでは、東部沿岸地域で「イングランド人」を選んだ人が多く、ニュースに登場したキャンベイ島を含むキャッスル・ポイントが77.5％で最高の割合でした。ウェールズでは、南部渓谷地域で「ウェールズ人」を選んだ人が多くなっています。ところが、年齢層を見てみると、イングランドやスコットランドと異なり、24歳以下の若年層（62％）の方が、25～64歳の人々（55％）よりも、「ウェールズ人」を選んだ率が高いことがわかりました。この背景には、近年の学校教育におけるウェールズ語学習の必修化があるようです。そして、スコットランドでは、中部地域で70％以上の人々が「スコットランド人」のアイデンティティを選びました。

　移民の増加などで、イギリスでは今後ますます「イギリス人」を名乗る人種的少数派が増えていくと思われます。「イングランド人」がその存在を危ぶまれる日も、そう遠くないかもしれません。

参考：http://www.ons.gov.uk/ons/guide-method/census/2011/index.html
　　　http://www.bbc.co.uk/news/magazine-12324970

5 Filling Gaps

CD2-17 [Original] CD2-18 [Voiced]

Watch the DVD, then fill the gaps in the text.

Newsreader: How British is Britain? New (¹   ) of the census reveals that working-age adults are much more likely to say they're British than pensioners. Just over 13% of the over-75s (²   ) themselves as British. And just 14% of white Britons (³   ) themselves as British. Here's our home editor, Mark Easton, with more.

Mark Easton: This is the most English place in England. In the last (⁴   ), for the first time, people were asked to describe their national (⁵   ). And on Canvey Island, eight out of ten people chose English, the highest proportion anywhere.

Easton: Why England and not Britain?

Man 1: Er, because I'm English and, um, I don't think, um, Britain is Britain anymore. Britain is, um, three or four different countries now.

Man 2: Look around you. There's so much (⁶   ). You know, will you get the same patriotism out of the (⁷   ) (⁸   )?

Easton: The census invited people to choose their identity. For example: English or Welsh? Do you see yourself as British or a mixture? The results show in England six out of ten people say simply English. In Wales and Scotland a similar (⁹   ) say Welsh and Scottish. But does that mean that Britishness is (¹⁰   )? Intriguingly, older people are less likely to say they're British than the young. The (¹¹   ) that watched the sun set on the Empire are the least likely of all to say they're Brits.

Man 3: If anybody said, 'Well, what (¹²   )'re you?' I would say English.

Woman 1: People who live in Wales and Scotland call themselves Welsh and Scottish so, so I feel that, that I'm English.

Easton: If the British identity was really a museum piece, how come young people choose it more than their grandparents? The answer to that may be found in the most (¹³   ) place in Britain: Harrow. But it's nothing to do with

Winston Churchill's old school. The explanation is (¹⁴   ). Among those whose (¹⁵   ) is white British, only 14% would say their identity is British, while almost half the black (¹⁶   ) would describe themselves that way. And the most British of all ... the (¹⁷   ). Fifty-six per cent pick British as their sole identity.

Easton: Would you ever say you were English?

Young woman 1: I have never said I'm English, no. I'm Brit-..., I still class myself as British, Indian.

Young woman 2: I think English, you kind of (¹⁸   ) (¹⁹   ), um, classify that as, um, white ethnic majority, whereas Britain tends to be a bit more multicultural, I would say.

Easton: Scottish bagpipes at an (²⁰   ) wedding in North London. What could be more British than that? In our increasingly (²¹   ) society, it seems the British identity finds itself quite at home. Mark Easton, BBC News.

(*Monday 30 September 2013*)

Notes

l. 1: **How British is Britain?**「(今) イギリスで、自分を『イギリス人』であると認識している人がどれだけいるでしょうか。」(「イギリスはどれだけイギリス色があるのでしょうか」が直訳)　イギリス (Britain) の正式名称はthe United Kingdom of Great Britain and Northern Irelandで、4つの国 (England, Scotland, Wales, Northern Ireland) から成り、イギリス国民は国籍としては本来"British"である　l. 3: **working-age adults**「就労年齢［生産年齢］の成人」 l. 12: **Canvey Island**「キャンベイ島」イングランド東部のエセックス州にある　l. 16: **three or four different countries** イギリスの上記4国のうち、ウェールズは早くにイングランドに併合された歴史があり、イングランドの一部と考える見方もある　l. 25: **the Empire**「(大英)帝国」 l. 29: **If the British identity was~** 文法的にはIf the British identity is~とすべきところ　l. 29: **a museum piece**「過去の遺物」 l. 31: **Harrow**「ハロー」大ロンドン北西部の区　l. 32: **Winston Churchill**「ウィンストン・チャーチル (1874-1965)」イギリスの政治家。1940-45年、1951-55年に首相を務める　l. 42: **class**「(~と) みなす」 l. 43: **British, Indian** ここは2語を分けて「イギリス人でありインド人」という、2つのナショナル・アイデンティティをもつと答えていると考えられる一方で、"British-Indian"（インド系イギリス人）と答えているとも解釈できる。話し手のイントネーションからは両方の可能性が考えられる　l. 47: **What could be more British than that?**「これ以上に『イギリスらしい』状況がありますか。」 l. 49: **finds itself quite at home**「(ふさわしい定義づけに) 居心地よくなじんでいる」

Behind the Scenes

ナショナル・アイデンティティ―両立は可能？

2012年のロンドン・オリンピックで、イギリス選手団の旗手を務めたのは自転車競技選手でスコットランド出身のクリス・ホイ（Chris Hoy）でした。ユニオン・ジャックを掲げて誇らしげに行進した彼は、金メダルを取った後にこのように述べています。

「私はスコットランド人であり、イギリス人です…この二つは矛盾するものではないのです」

「イギリスらしさ」は「スコットランドらしさ」や「イングランドらしさ」などと対立する概念のようにとらえられています。しかし、この二つは両立不可能ではありませんし、区別できるものでもありません。この年、女王の即位60周年記念に行われた映画に関する調査で、イギリス映画ナンバーワンに選ばれたのは、スコットランドを舞台とし、登場人物たちがスコットランドの方言で話す『トレインスポッティング』でした。このように、「イギリスらしさ」とそれぞれの地域のアイデンティティは、時に重なり合いながら存在しているのです。

▶▶▶ Moving On

6 Making a Summary

CD2-19

Fill the gaps to complete the summary.

The most recent census of the British population has shown that most people, and particularly older pensioners, say that their national (i   ) is not British, but English or Welsh. On Canvey Island, for example, 80% of the people call themselves English. One man said that this is because ethnic (m   ) have less (p   ). One reason why younger people are more likely to call themselves British is that there is more (d   ) among them, and people whose (e   ) is not 'white British' tend to (i   ) themselves as British. Two young women from Indian families who described themselves as British said that this was because they felt that 'English' sounded less (m   ) than 'British'. A good example of British (c   ) society is Scottish bagpipes playing at an Indian wedding in North London.

7 Follow Up

Discuss, write or present.

1. Do you think there is any difference in national identity between young people and old people in Japan?
2. London is one of the most cosmopolitan cities in the world, with a diverse population and many people with different ethnic backgrounds. Do you think this is a good thing? How does London compare with Tokyo?
3. Do you think ethnic minorities are likely to be less patriotic?

Unit 15
A New Gateway for Immigrants?

不法移民の多くが今やギリシャからヨーロッパに入っているようです。ギリシャの抱える移民問題、また厳しい状況から逃れてきた移民の現状について学びましょう。

▶ Starting Off

1 Setting the Scene

What do you think?

1. Does Japan have a problem with illegal immigration?
2. What do you think are the five largest immigrant groups in Japan?

2 Building Language

Which word (1-5) best fits which explanation (a-e)?

1. frontier [ ]   a. deal with a situation effectively
2. perilous [ ]   b. run away from danger
3. cope   [ ]   c. border separating two countries
4. influx [ ]   d. arrival of large numbers of people or things
5. flee   [ ]   e. very dangerous, risky

85

▶▶ **Watching the News**

3 Understanding Check 1

Read the quotes, then watch the DVD and match them to the right people.

1. Until last year, 90% of illegal immigrants entered Europe through Greece. [ ]

2. They are going away from a difficult situation and they just need to be supported. [ ]

3. We have to protect from the criminal networks. [ ]

4. Since police increased controls on the land border with Turkey... [ ]

4 Understanding Check 2

Which is the best answer?

1. Why are the Greek islands now bearing the brunt of illegal immigration?
   a. The islands are easier to get to.
   b. Police have increased controls on the land border with Turkey.
   c. More boats are travelling to the islands.
   d. The Greek economy is improving.

2. Why are so many immigrants travelling from Syria?
   a. They are fleeing the war.
   b. Syria is having an economic crisis.
   c. Wages are low in Syria.
   d. Syria has many natural disasters.

3. Approximately, how many migrants have tried to cross the water to get to Lesvos this year?
   a. 1,300
   b. 366
   c. 90
   d. 4,500

What do you remember?

4. How many migrants died trying to reach the island of Lampedusa?

_____

5. Why is Greece struggling to cope with the influx of illegal immigrants?

_____

6. How much did the young Syrians each pay to get to Europe?

_____

●●Background Information●●

　今回のニュースで話題になったギリシャへの不法移民の多くは、シリアからの難民です。2011年3月にシリアで内戦が始まって以来、シリアの人口約2190万人の4割以上に当たる、約900万人のシリア人が国内、もしくは隣国へ避難しました。UNHCR（国連難民高等弁務官事務所）によると、約250万人がレバノン（約86万人）、ヨルダン（約58万人）、トルコ（約56万人）、イラク（約21万人）、エジプト（約13万人）へ移住し、約650万人がシリア国内での移住を余儀なくされています。

　一方、欧米に保護を求めたシリア人は10万人以下とされています。2013年から14年にかけてのシリア難民の最大受け入れ国はアメリカで、その人数は無制限、次いでドイツが11000人、カナダ1300人、スウェーデン1200人、ノルウェー1000人と続き、その他の国々は500人以下の難民受け入れを約束しました。

　イギリスはというと、政府はUNHCRの活動に協力することを拒み、難民の受け入れに否定的な見解を示しています。その理由として、イギリス政府は、シリア国内での紛争の解決と難民が居住地に戻ることを優先課題としている、と述べています。その一方で政府は、6億ポンドの支援と、女性や子供、高齢者など弱い立場の人々の数百人規模のイギリスへの受け入れを表明しています。

参考：http://www.bbc.com/news/uk-politics-25934659
　　　http://syrianrefugees.eu/

5 Filling Gaps

CD2-20 [Original]   CD2-21 [Voiced]

Watch the DVD, then fill the gaps in the text.

Newsreader: It is almost a month since 366 migrants died trying to (¹   ) the Italian island of Lampedusa. But now it is Greece, as well as Italy, which is becoming one of Europe's key immigration (²   ). Until last year, 90% of illegal immigrants entered Europe through Greece. The numbers are falling, but the Greek government says it is still shouldering a huge (³   ) in the midst of a deep economic (⁴   ). So far this year, nearly four and a half thousand people, many of them (⁵   ) the war in Syria, have squeezed into overcrowded dinghies to make the (⁶   ) journey to the Turkish mainland, from where they then (⁷   ) the six miles to the Greek island of Lesvos. Our correspondent, Mark Lowen, is on the island. Mark.

Mark Lowen: The vast Aegean, where the hopes of reaching Europe still burn (⁸   ). We're on patrol with the Greek coastguard off Lesvos Island, combing the EU's south-east (⁹   ) for illegal immigrants. It's a key gateway and a perilous journey, but numbers are soaring.

Lt Antonios Sofiadelis, Lesvos Coastguard: I hope and I will ask for more (¹⁰   ) from EU member states, er, but that doesn't mean that we're going to stop. If this help, if this assistance doesn't come, we have to protect our, our (¹¹   ). We have to protect from the criminal networks.

Lowen: It's a now (¹²   ) scene, overcrowded boats docking here recently. They are the lucky ones who (¹³   ) it. Plenty don't and Greece says Europe must do more.

Lowen: This year alone almost four and a half thousand migrants have tried to cross these waters into Lesvos. Since police increased controls on the land border with Turkey, it's now the islands bearing the brunt. And Greece, in the midst of its worst economic crisis in living memory, with (¹⁴   ) already stretched beyond limit, is struggling to (¹⁵   ) with the (¹⁶   ).

Evi Latsoudi, Doctors of the World: I feel (^{17}). I feel a shame when they talk to us about the problems they have and they face in my country, and I feel very angry because I believe we can (^{18}) something and we don't. Most of them, they are like us. They are going away from a difficult situation and they just need to be supported.

Lowen: At the ferry to Athens we met some young Syrians. They paid 1,300 euros each to get to Europe.

Immigrant from Syria: My family doesn't want his son die with, in in his eyes. So my family say go out, go out, go out from Syria. I'm looking for a free life, to be myself, to (^{19}) myself first and go back to Syria.

Lowen: All they have is one bag and their dreams. How many more will (^{20}) in their wake before the tide of immigration is stemmed?

(Thursday 31 October 2013)

Notes ·······

l. 2: **migrants**「(来たばかりの) 移民」 l. 3: **Lampedusa**「ランペドゥーサ」地中海のイタリア領の島 l. 7: **immigrants**「(永住を目的とした外国からの) 移民」 l. 14: **Lesvos**「レスボス島」エーゲ海東部、トルコの北西沖にあるギリシャ領の島。Lesbos (レスボス島) の現代ギリシャ語名。Lesvosの綴りでは「レズボス島」とすべきだが、「レスボス島」の呼称が一般的 l. 15: **Aegean**「エーゲ海」ギリシャとトルコ間の地中海の一部 l. 17: **combing**「(を求めて) 徹底的に捜査している」 l. 27: **waters**「海」複数形で使われるときの意味に注意 l. 28: **bearing the brunt**「矢面に立っています」(移民の入り口として) 矢面に立っているということ l. 35: **a shame** ashamedとするのが一般的 l. 44: **My family doesn't want his son die with, in in his eyes.** 本来ならMy family don't want to see me die. となるべきところ l. 48: **in their wake**「(〜が) 通った跡 [道]」

Behind the Scenes

移民たちの移動手段

移民たちの移動手段として利用されるのはボートだけではありません。2013年10月、アフリカのニジェールからアルジェリアを経由しヨーロッパを目指していた移民92人が、サハラ砂漠で遺体で発見されました。車の故障で砂漠に取り残されたと考えられています。また、飛行機の車輪の格納庫に隠れる手段もしばしば見られますが、格納庫は気温の調整がされないため、飛行中に凍死するケースがほとんどです。電車、バスを使って国境を越えようとする人々も多くいます。また、何の輸送手段も使わず、歩いたり、海や川を泳いで国境を越えようとしたりする場合もあります。どの手段をとるにせよ、国境を越えることは容易ではありません。しかしながら、ヨーロッパの国同士で移民を押し付け合う行為も見られる現在、移民たちは移動することを余儀なくされているのです。

▶▶▶ Moving On

6 Making a Summary

CD2-22

Fill the gaps to complete the summary.

Large numbers of illegal (i   ) are entering Europe, and a small Greek island is becoming one of Europe's key immigration (f   ). This is because police have increased their controls on the land border with Turkey. So now, many people, (f   ) the war in Syria, make the (p   ) journey in (o   ) dinghies to the Greek island of Lesvos. The Greek coastguard wants more help from EU member states. Greece is in the (m   ) of a serious economic crisis, and is struggling to (c   ) with the (i   ) of so many immigrants entering Europe in the hope of finding a better life.

7 Follow Up

Discuss, write or present.

1. Would you like Japan to have closer ties with its neighbouring countries?
2. What is your opinion of Japan's immigration policy?
3. How does Japan deal with refugees and asylum-seekers? Read about refugees in Japan at this website: http://www.refugee.or.jp/, then give your opinion about it.

本書にはCD（別売）があります

Seeing the World through the News 2
DVDで学ぶイギリス国営放送の英語 2

2015年1月20日　初版第1刷発行
2015年9月25日　初版第3刷発行

編著者　　Timothy Knowles
　　　　　Daniel Brooks
　　　　　武　岡　由樹子
　　　　　田　村　真　弓
　　　　　浦　口　理　麻

発行者　　福　岡　正　人
発行所　　株式会社　金　星　堂
（〒101-0051）東京都千代田区神田神保町 3-21
　　　　Tel. (03)3263-3828（営業部）
　　　　　　 (03)3263-3997（編集部）
　　　　Fax (03)3263-0716
　　　　http://www.kinsei-do.co.jp

編集担当　長島吉成　　　　　　　　Printed in Japan
印刷所・製本所／三美印刷株式会社
本書の無断複製・複写は著作権法上での例外を除き禁じられています。本書を代行業者等の第三者に依頼してスキャンやデジタル化することは、たとえ個人や家庭内での利用であっても認められておりません。
落丁・乱丁本はお取り替えいたします。

ISBN978-4-7647-3996-3 C1082